# Preparing Sons

## to Provide for a Single-Income Family

D1462528

*Steven Maxwell*

 CCI Communication Concepts, Inc.

Preparing Sons to Provide for a Single-Income Family

Ordering information:
Managers of Their Homes
2416 South 15th Street
Leavenworth, Kansas 66048
Phone: (913) 772-0392
Web: www.Titus2.com

Published by:
Communication Concepts, Inc.
www.we-communicate.com


ACKNOWLEDGEMENTS

Scripture taken from the HOLY BIBLE, KING JAMES VERSION.

ISBN 0-9669107-3-7

Printed in the United States of America

1 2 3

This book was created in Microsoft Word. QuarkXPress 4.1 and Adobe Photoshop 6.0 were used for layout and design. All computers were Windows based systems running Windows NT/2000.

Cover design by Christopher Maxwell and inside design by Sarah Maxwell.

This book is dedicated to:

All the homeschooling fathers who are willing to sacrifice their free time, pleasure, and entertainment and to invest that time in their young men.

# Contents

---

# Acknowledgments

---

I am very grateful for the loving support and many hours of work given me by my family in the final stages of *Preparing Sons*. My first and greatest assistance came from the helpmeet God has given me. My wife, Teri, spent countless hours in critiquing, editing, and revising.

Sarah laid out the book, and her keen eye was very helpful in proofreading. The years Teri spent with Christopher teaching sentence analysis were invaluable as he was skillful in doing the first-round text edits. We chose Christopher's cover design over Joseph's. (Maybe next time, Joseph. Keep learning, working, and trying!)

A thank you goes to three others as well. My former pastor, dear friend, and brother in Christ, Richard C. Seim, D. Min., was my "technical" editor. Tim Cahill, another friend and brother in Christ, read through the manuscript in one weekend, offering helpful suggestions. Also a man whom I respect greatly, Dr. S. M. Davis, provided last minute comments and encouragement.

And finally, a special thank you to David Barton for taking the time to research and answer my e-mail many months ago. I was seeking objective feedback as to whether history affirmed the premise of this book, and his response was a great encouragement to me.

# Preface

As the father of five boys, I have felt the responsibility of rais-ing sons who could one day provide for their families without their wives needing outside-the-home employment. This respon-sibility became even keener when we began homeschooling in 1985. No longer was I able to rely on a school system to prepare my sons for their futures as wage-earning adults.

The principles and suggestions presented in this book have come from my study of Scripture, my own experiences in raising two of my sons to adulthood, plus personal observations of other men and their sons. As my wife, Teri, and I walked through the years of our children's lives, we did not have a plan or formula in mind such as I lay out before you in this book. However, we did have God's Word, which we turned to constantly for direction and encouragement.

I want to introduce you to my children since they are key players in the chapters you will be reading. It is impossible for me to write without using personal examples. My own children are the best illustrations I have of some of the points I am making. At the time of the writing of this book, here is what my family "looks" like:

My wife, Teri

| | |
|---|---|
| Nathan - age 24 | John - age 10 |
| Christopher - age 22 | Anna - age 8 |
| Sarah - age 19 | Jesse - age 6 |
| Joseph - age 12 | Mary - age 4 |

Please understand that this book is written from a decidedly Christian point of view. Because of my love for Jesus Christ and the dedication of my life to Him, I am not able to write anything that does not use the Bible as its foundation and starting point. You will find Scripture quotes throughout.

Don't expect this book to tell you what vocation to have your son prepare for or whether he should go to college or not. However, it is designed to set out guidelines and suggestions for helping you and your son make these decisions. You will find practical ideas, starting with the preschool years and going up through early adulthood, that will be applicable for preparing your son for whatever vocation the Lord calls him to.

Please don't leave this book on the shelf until your son is a senior in high school. The time to begin laying the foundations that will help him support a one-income family begins in his preschool and elementary years. While parents who have missed this particular direction for those early years can catch up, don't miss it if your children are still very young!

It is my desire that as you read this book you will be filled with an excitement over the prospect of preparing your son to provide for a single-income family. I want you to see the possibilities and then purposefully set out to meet them. I hope you will begin to view each aspect of your son's life as having an impact on his ability to support a family one day. I would like for you to own your responsibility in this process and to face it with seriousness and anticipation.

*Steve Maxwell*

---

An hour's industry will do more to produce cheerful-
ness, suppress evil humors, and retrieve your
affairs, than a month's moaning. Sloth makes all
things difficult, but industry all easy.
*Benjamin Franklin*

I believe that withholding children from work
will benefit neither the family, the child, nor
the adult that the child will become.
*David Barton*

---

# Providing for a Single-Income Family

---

*The labour of the righteous tendeth to life.*
*Proverbs 10:16*

---

We have known Troy for many years. As a homeschooled student in high school, his first job was as a two-week temporary assistant to the most junior employee in the company. Troy was hired to move heavy archive boxes in the basement. Since this was his first real job, Troy determined to do his best regardless of how menial the tasks. Hauling boxes doesn't sound like an impressive start to a career, does it? However, it was amazing to see how God was working. While doing his work assignments, Troy was diligent in learning the archiving system of the company. He also tried to perform each task quickly so he would be available to do other "little" things for his boss.

His temporary position was extended, and after a couple of months, he replaced his "boss" as archiving manager for the company. Throughout the next year or so, he completely redesigned the archive system from the bottom up. This included designing a new database and tracking system for more than 4,000 boxes of information.

Computers have always interested Troy, and he found himself helping various people in the company with small projects in his spare time. While not an expert in formulas or the financial aspects of spreadsheets, his desire to learn enabled him to create, fix, and modify spreadsheets. Thus he began to be used in the process of converting the company's spreadsheets from Lotus 1-2-3 to Microsoft Excel. After a while he was doing spreadsheet and database consulting full time. He completely redesigned the company's largest financial spreadsheet (which was made up of seventeen inter-working spreadsheets) in a three-month-long development project.

Troy began working for minimum wage, and while still in high school his hourly rate had climbed to twenty-five dollars per hour. Our experience has been similar. I have seen that if a young man is prepared properly, he will excel in the workplace.

Training a son to provide for a one-income family begins long before he writes his first resume hoping to be hired for a full-time job! The skills, character, education, and spiritual foundation necessary for supporting his family will be established throughout his childhood. As a parent, you will be the most important factor in your son's preparation for his future as a wage earner. Are you ready for this task?

I have yet to meet parents who don't want the best for their children. That is certainly a wonderful, God-given desire. As you raise your children, you are making decisions that will affect them for the rest of their lives. Do you ever have concerns as to whether you have made right or wrong decisions?

Some of these decisions have far greater consequences than others. Maybe a child wanted to quit playing a musical instrument, and you let him stop. What will that mean ten years from now? If a son didn't want to pursue a foreign language or a difficult math course, what are the ramifications of that choice during his lifetime?

Of even greater concern might be decisions regarding whether a child pursues higher education. What if you don't have the funds to put your son through post–high school education? Will you have ruined his chances of success in life? Is a checkbook the only meaningful way parents can help? How can you prepare a son to support a family?

## Two Are Better Than One—Unless You Mean Two Incomes

Most of us have seen moms at the grocery store with children who are terrors. Observing those children makes me thankful for a wife who is able to devote all of her time to nurturing our children. As a result, I have never been concerned about taking my five youngest children with me on an errand. Teri's folks have expressed similar gratefulness that they are able to take our children anywhere without fear of making a scene. They report the children are always well behaved for them.

Raising godly children is a difficult, full-time job. It takes a great deal of time and effort. Will your future daughter-in-law be able to stay home with the children, or will she have to work full time? Will she want to stay home with the children?

The answers to those questions will likely be determined by how you raise your son and by the values you impress on his life. This affects the type of woman he is attracted to for his wife. In addition, it has much to do with the type of leadership he provides for his home. We must purpose to instill in our sons the desire to have their wives home nurturing their children. Now is the time to be working with our sons and developing them according to God's Word and His leading.

## The Cast

Through the years I have had the opportunity to observe many people working in their vocation. It is no surprise why some do well in life while others do not.

I have renamed a partial list of characters who will be referred to throughout the book. These are real people whom I have known personally with their names and details modified to protect their privacy. As you read the following biographical profiles, evaluate each man and see if you can spot why he didn't do as well as he could have or what factors made him successful. We will look at each example in depth later in the book. For now, see what you glean from reading these snapshots.

Bob is one of the hardest working men I have ever known. He worked two jobs to support his family. He fell into bed at 1 a.m., having to rise for work again by 6 a.m. During this time, his teenage daughter gave birth out of wedlock, and his son found himself in serious trouble with the law.

Kevin is a good worker but known to be somewhat moody. If you ever want to snap him out of a bad mood, bring up duck hunting or bass fishing. They are his passions! He admits to having a good marriage as long as he doesn't spend too much time with his wife. If they are together for long, they begin to argue. Therefore, he spends all of his free time hunting, fishing, or maintaining his sports gear.

Larry tried college after high school but then quit. He worked in his parents' business for several years until it closed. His income averages one hundred thousand dollars a year as a self-taught programmer. His wife is home full time with their large family. They give everything that he earns over their needs to missionaries.

Eric had his own graphic design business for two years. He loved throwing his heart into making it successful. Unfortunately, he would have starved had he not been living with his parents. His father wanted to teach Eric programming, but Eric only had eyes for graphic design and wasn't interested.

Herb is a professional with an advanced degree, a wife, several small children, and an extremely good income. He eagerly became involved in a pyramid marketing business. The goal was to work less and have more income. Neither resulted.

David has a four-year college degree and just received an excellent job offer from another company. However, it would mean moving his family away from extended family, longtime friends, and the church that they love.

Steve has an electrical engineering degree. He spent twenty years in good corporate jobs. The last three years of his corporate work, Steve's oldest, homeschooled son, who had not gone to college, earned a significantly larger salary than his father.

Dave has an automotive repair facility near our town. It is small, but he has a reputation for being honest and doing good work. He learned the trade from his father and never attended college. His shop has been an excellent source of income, and he appears to lack for nothing.

Scott paints houses for a living. He is well known for his quality work. He has a large family, and even though his work is seasonal, he doesn't struggle financially. I have never known anyone else on whom God's hand of blessing so clearly rests.

Sid has a four-year degree and a reputation as a diligent worker. He received promotions and increased responsibility while he was with his company. When he first hired on, the salary was low enough that it was a struggle for his family to make ends meet. However, in time his promotions included significant pay increases due to the value others placed on his participation. He is one of the most overt witnesses for Jesus Christ I have ever seen.

Dan was eager to tell others in his company about Jesus. He earned a reasonable wage that met the needs of his family. However, Dan had a reputation for not getting his work done. He was always willing to spend lots of company time discussing just about anything in the hopes of winning people to Christ.

## What to Expect

What benefit can you expect from reading this book? You should first form an understanding of the real issues that affect a son's ability to provide for his family. Then you should come to see what God has to say about these difficulties and what your responsibility is in it all.

You should find this book practical, encouraging, and full of real-life examples. Three of my eight children are wage-earning adults and well prepared for life. I share from Scripture, my family's lives, my heart, and my personal observations regarding the wonderful responsibility that is ours as parents to train sons who are able to provide for a one-income family.

This book is "anti" doing something just because it is the popular choice. I am going to challenge you to make the best possible decisions based on God's leading so that your son will be able to provide for his family. Keep in mind, though, good family providers don't occur simply because everyone else is "doing it"!

God has given parents the opportunity to impact their children in a most wonderful way for the rest of their lives. You can, with God's direction, raise sons who are able to provide for their families!

## Questions

1. Have you begun considering your son's future in the working world?

2. What do you envision him doing vocationally?

3. What do you see your role to be in preparing him for his future?

4. What strengths do you have that will help in this preparation?

5. What weaknesses do you have that will hinder in this preparation?

6. What do you imagine will be your greatest challenge in preparing your son?

7. Do you see yourself represented in any of the cast?

---

Idleness is the parent of every vice. Labor
of all kinds favors and facilitates the practice
of virtue. It is a common saying, make men
work and you will make them honest.

*Benjamin Rush*

Opportunity is missed by most people because
it is dressed in overalls and looks like work.

*Thomas A. Edison*

---

# What Is His
# Earning Potential?

---

*In all labour there is profit: but the*
*talk of the lips tendeth only to penury.*
*Proverbs 14:23*

---

Are there factors that come into play concerning our sons'
earning potential that we as parents would be wise to be attentive
to? I believe that you will agree the following areas are very important in determining your son's future income. Your son will greatly benefit from your careful attention to them.

## Vocation

A man's vocation is generally what we think determines how
much money he makes. If you meet a visitor at church and find
out he is a doctor or lawyer, you will likely think, "Here is someone with few financial difficulties." On the other hand, when we
think of firemen, pastors, policemen, and schoolteachers, we don't
picture them making huge salaries.

It seems like every son wants to be a fireman, policeman, or
bulldozer operator at some point in his young life. Then as he
matures, other jobs catch his interest. Just because a person is
interested in a profession doesn't mean it is right for him.

You can have a great deal of influence on your son's future vocation by what you say to him concerning those vocations. It isn't a matter of trying to manipulate our sons' interest into high-paying careers, but rather of encouraging them according to God's leading. As you observe God's gifting of talent in your son's life and as you seek the Lord to find out how He wants to use that son, the Lord will begin making His way known to both of you.

Christopher, my second oldest son, was near the point of making a commitment to a vocation. He was very interested in pursuing EMT credentials to become an emergency medical technician. I wondered if his engrossment was mostly due to an excitement factor connected with EMT work. In addition, Christopher has a very strong leading toward raising a family some day. Christopher and I discussed and prayed about his vocation decision. We also discussed the fact that EMTs have to work odd shifts, and it is very common for a man and woman to be paired up. Having to work alone with a woman all day or night can lead to unhealthy temptation. The odd shifts also bring added difficulty to a family and would often disrupt a daily schedule. Over time, Christopher could see that raising a family and being an EMT might bring problems to his marriage and family that would be prudent to avoid. "A prudent *man* foreseeth the evil, and hideth himself: but the simple pass on, and are punished" (Proverbs 22:3). I was pleased that Christopher saw the wisdom of pursuing a different career, even though it might be less exciting.

Please don't misunderstand me. Through my illustration, I am not saying a Christian can't have an EMT type of job. I am saying that it is wise to count the cost beforehand. You as the parent have the opportunity to present realistic considerations to your son as he is evaluating and praying about his future vocation.

A child may also express interest in a career that Christians should not even consider such as owning a nightclub, movie rental store, abortion facility, or liquor store. It is possible his spiritual maturity is insufficient to recognize something as wrong. That is where a parent can help him see God's will more clearly. Take him directly to Scripture to support your claims. The verses you use would make excellent Bible study topics for you and your son.

The career that our sons choose will clearly impact their ability to provide for their families. We've briefly looked at vocations; now we will look at two of the primary ways your son will qualify for those vocations: education and skill level.

## Education

Education is usually thought of next when it comes to determining the size of an income. I have seen studies correlating the number of years a person attends school to their income. In general, with God out of the equation, I believe that is true. However, more education does not necessarily mean higher incomes. I wonder how often the decision to send a child to school somewhere is based on the parent's fear that the child will not succeed unless he goes. Educational goals should never be based on fear. Rather, these goals should always be determined through careful discernment of God's direction for the child.

Training and education possibilities seem to be limitless. Do we enroll or send our children to every training opportunity? Of course not. We should prayerfully consider each "opportunity" before our children participate. We need to realize that we are in essence entering into a buyer/seller relationship each time we write a check for training. The money you are going to give the sellers motivates them. Your children's best interests may not necessarily be their first consideration. Most likely, the training institution's primary concern is paying their bills; therefore, they need students paying tuition. We must be very careful, shrewd customers anytime we are purchasing training for our children.

Remember Steve, mentioned in Chapter One? That is me. If I had wanted a larger income, should I have pursued a master's degree? Yes, if I was to believe the commercials on the radio. However, that was not God's leading and not consistent with my abilities. Would I have made more money had I earned a master's? Only the Lord knows for sure, but with my limited math and science abilities, I doubt I would have justified the higher wages that a master's degree would have brought. As a result, I might have been discouraged, and the company employing me would not have felt they were getting their money's worth.

Something else to consider is that those with higher degrees may experience difficulty finding jobs. The work force is like a pyramid in that the higher you climb the education ladder, the fewer jobs you'll find requiring those skills. That is why it is imperative that the parents know God's direction for their child. Overconfidence may lead to disappointment when a degree does not bring the anticipated salary. In fact, I have heard people calling Christian radio talk shows complaining about how difficult it is to repay their student loan based on the amount of money they are currently making. They had expected a higher salary upon graduating with a degree.

I have spoken with many telemarketers over the years. One day I spoke with a young telemarketer who was selling computer products. He mentioned he had a degree in marketing. I couldn't believe it! When I questioned him, he said he wasn't able to find other employment after he graduated. His plan was to continue in the telemarketing position for several years and then try for a better job. He acknowledged his job paid poorly, and at this point his degree was of little benefit.

A few weeks ago our family was shopping at a chain home-improvement store. The man who was helping us had a degree in elementary education. He said he was trying out some other jobs to see what he wanted to do with his life.

Hopefully, you are beginning to see that the number of years your son is educated can be a factor in what he earns for his family, but there is much more to it than that. We must seek the Lord for His specific direction for each child.

## Skill Level

When Joseph was a toddler, he developed a cough that wouldn't go away. We had just moved to Kansas, so we took him to a doctor we picked out of the telephone book. The physician was in his sixties and very personable. However, he had great difficulty looking in Joseph's throat as Joseph was not being very cooperative. After several attempts, he appeared to give up but said he had seen enough to give us a prescription. Teri and I were confident he had not been successful in seeing Joseph's throat, and we felt that he was guessing at a diagnosis. After a couple of weeks with no improvement, we took Joseph to another doctor who promptly diagnosed and successfully treated him. Later we spoke with others who had tried the first doctor, and they too had opted for someone else.

Here was a doctor, with plenty of credentials and schooling, who should have been making a good salary. However, his skill level was poor. I don't know what his actual income might have been, but if the condition of his office and the lack of patients was any indication, the man was not making much money at all.

On the other hand, you will remember Dave, the mechanic I mentioned in Chapter One. He is skilled and even though there is no lack of mechanics in our area, he appears to be making a very good living.

How skilled a person is at their work will have a significant impact on their income level. It is not sufficient to have accomplished "x" number of years of education and hold a job in a particular vocation, we must also be good at what we do.

We should instill in our children the necessity of always doing their best. "And whatsoever ye do, do *it* heartily, as to the Lord, and not unto men" (Colossians 3:23).

## The Parent's Responsibility

As a parent, you will have great influence on the vocation your son chooses, the education he pursues, and his skill level. This is an awesome responsibility to shoulder. Much prayer is necessary on your part as you contemplate the discussions you will have with your son on these topics and the counsel you will give to him.

Later chapters in this book address the specifics of preparing your son for his vocation, building his skill level, and directing him in his educational choices. For now keep in mind that the three areas we have just discussed—vocation, education, and skill level—are what most people primarily consider when evaluating earning potential. It is true that they have an impact on the size of a man's income. However, it is important that we realize that there is more to the equation.

## Questions

1.  What correlation do you observe between vocation and income?

2.  Are there vocations you would like to steer your son away from? Why? Can you support this Biblically?

3.  How important is education to your son's ability to provide for a one-income family? Why?

4.  Thinking back on your education, has it helped increase your income? Would you do anything differently?

5.  How do you view skill level affecting a man's income?

---

The labour of the righteous
*tendeth* to life . . . (Proverbs 10:16)

. . . but he that gathereth by labour
shall increase. (Proverbs 13:11)

In all labour there is
profit . . . (Proverbs 14:23)

And also that every man should
eat and drink, and enjoy the
good of all his labour, it *is*
the gift of God. (Ecclesiastes 3:13)

The sleep of a labouring man
*is* sweet . . . (Ecclesiastes 5:12)

We must renew our thinking to conform
to the messages of these verses, which
may mean that we must learn to
change our attitude about work.
*David Barton*

---

# What Is His REAL Earning Potential?

---

*Wealth gotten by vanity shall be diminished:
but he that gathereth by labour shall increase.
Proverbs 13:11*

---

Who would ever have believed that a young homeschool graduate could make as much money as his college-degreed father? Who might guess that the same son would be paid to write an instructor's manual for college professors teaching computer security? This is exactly what happened in our family!

While we generally think about vocation, education, and skill level in reference to earning potential, other factors can have a powerful, if not even greater, influence as well. You will see how you, the parent, are key in modeling these ingredients for your son and training him in them.

## View of Work

When I worked for Boeing, Jerry was on my team. He was close to sixty years old and held a four-year engineering degree. Jerry was a genius. Unfortunately, no one wanted him on their team, as the man would not complete a task. Normal, mundane work was an incredible bore to him because he had a multitude of side interests that were always more important than his work. As a result of his poor work habits, Jerry only received token wage increases. He viewed work as a necessary evil to be put up with in order to receive a paycheck. His check was a ticket to the toys that made his life worth living.

At one point, it sounded like Jerry was going to be fired. However, as a last ditch effort, Boeing transferred him to a job that involved solving problems for the production lines. Finally, they had found a job that interested Jerry enough to keep him motivated. As a result, Jerry and everyone around him were happier. If Jerry had viewed work as a gift from God and something to be greatly prized, he wouldn't have come so close to being fired. Plus, he would have been receiving pay increases through the years like others.

Jerry is one of many I have known who had an awful view of work. Not only did they not perform well for their company, they were a plague that infected other employees. The employer's usual solution was to fire them. "Cast out the scorner, and contention shall go out; yea, strife and reproach shall cease" (Proverbs 22:10). Now that really affects one's income!

Parents should teach their children that work is a gift from God. Workers with that attitude are a pleasure to work with and will have a positive influence on other employees. Their job will be secure and their wages will increase. What are your children's attitudes regarding work? What will their work attitudes be ten years from now? We will discuss the specifics of developing a positive attitude toward work in your sons' lives in the chapters on training for particular ages.

## Character

In certain circles there is much talk about character. Character is probably the number one reason why families want to homeschool their children. They want to be able to properly develop their children's character. Whatever progress parents make in developing positive character will pay dividends throughout the life of a child.

Men who are diligent, honest, resourceful, dependable, and responsible workers will do well. These days there are so few such people in our society that employers are hungry for them. From talking with several employers, I have learned that character is often more important than skills and qualifications. Employers are willing to train a person who has good character as long as certification and degrees aren't a mandatory requirement for the job (for example, an engineering job).

Eddie had worked with Tommy for about a year. Eddie was aware that Tommy fraudulently recorded his time on the job, and later Eddie had to confront Tommy on some other ethical issues. Eddie naturally assumed that Tommy would have hard feelings toward him after the confrontation. Tommy ended up leaving the company and going to work somewhere else. Months later, Eddie was totally amazed to receive a job offer from the new company for which Tommy was working. Even more surprising was the story behind the offer. Tommy's new boss had asked him to recommend a person whom the boss would be able to trust explicitly. The job would involve sensitive computer security, and ethics were a great concern. Tommy told the boss that he could wholeheartedly recommend Eddie as that person!

There are no shortcuts to character. It will take much training, effort, and prayer by the parents to raise children of strong character. However, it will greatly affect your child's earning potential for the rest of his life.

## Eager to Learn

Years ago Larry was given the opportunity to learn computer programming at his job. They had a problem and needed help. Larry thought it sounded like a good opportunity and volunteered. However, his boss was a very demanding person and constantly "rode his back." The work was hard, the hours long, and Larry was often insulted. Any "normal" person would have been long gone. However, God did not direct Larry to leave, and he would not change jobs unless God told him to. In a small way the situation reminded Larry of Joseph's suffering in Egypt, and he was determined to persevere. In time, the boss left the company, and working conditions became more pleasant.

Today, as Larry looks back he is able to see how God used that time as a boot-camp learning experience for his own good. Larry's harsh boss was used by God to develop a strong work ethic in Larry. In fact, I don't know of a harder worker who pays more careful attention to detail than Larry. Larry wants God's best in his life and is willing to suffer to get it.

The Old Testament's Noah, Joseph, and Daniel would tell us that God's best is often not our first choice, especially if our emotions are making the choice. God's best does not cater to our flesh and so the flesh is rarely thrilled. By not being open to every learning experience He sends, we may miss out. "For as the heavens are higher than the earth, so are my ways higher than your ways and my thoughts than your thoughts" (Isaiah 55:9). A man who has a hungry soul is willing to be molded according to God's plan and wants God's will done, not his own.

## God's Blessing

After twenty years of corporate engineering work, I came home to start a family business. It was an agonizing decision because I wanted to be certain it was God's will. As much as I desired to work from our home, I was scared to do so it if it wasn't God's explicit will for my life. When I was confident it was His will, I came home. At first, I had only a vague idea of what I might do. I felt God was leading me to sell printing and computer forms. Christopher, who was eighteen at the time, was going to work with me.

We knew absolutely nothing about selling computer forms and printed materials, yet God led and blessed as we went. The Lord provided a friend in that same line of work who lived in another city and was willing to give us some ideas about starting a print brokering business. He also provided us with a list of companies that did wholesale printing for him, something of great value to us. Then we were on our own and probably should have failed miserably. We had no training, no experience, and no skill, but God blessed mightily by bringing work. We have now been in business four years. There have been many changes since we began. We experienced times without abundance, but our God has met every need. What a wonderful testimony to God's faithfulness! Yet, if we believe His Word, it should not be surprising at all.

We see in Scripture how God chose to bless Joseph, Daniel, and Jacob, and He will bless your sons as they walk with Him. When God blesses the work of a man's hands, he will prosper.

## God's Discipline

One final, very important factor I would like to discuss is God's discipline. No matter how perfect the vocation, education, and skill level are, if God chooses to administer discipline through a person's income, that man will suffer. In fact, anytime my family begins to experience financial difficulties, I immediately start asking the Lord if He is trying to get my attention.

In Deuteronomy 28:17 we read, "Cursed *shall be* thy basket and thy store." The context of this verse explains that the curse is judgment for disobedience. God will curse the gathering of food, wages, and even financial stores. As parents we need to instill a real fear of the Lord into our children. They must know that if they are saved, God desires to conform them to the image of His Son (Romans 8:29), and if the need arises, He will discipline them.

In 1985 we moved to Washington so I could become a salesman for my company. My previous job had been at the company's headquarters doing marketing, but I wanted a sales position because the money was far better. However, after a year of hard work, everything that could go wrong had! I began calling out to the Lord to show me what was wrong. I still remember the day He answered my prayer. Out of the blue, a vivid memory popped into mind. It was of the test I took to qualify for the sales position. This test was designed to compare my personality with the profile of the company's top salesmen. I recalled asking myself, as I completed that test, how the ace salesman would answer each question. Then I would write that answer down. It never occurred to me that I was being dishonest and, in effect, cheating.

My heart sank at the realization that I, as a child of God, had lied on a test. I felt awful and asked the Lord to forgive me. I knew I needed to resign, because I had obtained the job deceitfully. Immediately I began looking for another job, but God soon convicted me that I needed to quit my sales position first. I definitely did not like the idea of being without a job, but knew I had to obey. I went in and told my manager the story, explaining that I had to quit. It brings tears to my eyes as I remember her looking at me and saying I could take two full weeks with pay to look for a job. I didn't even need to come into work! I was flooded with such incredible joy and knew in my heart that I was back under God's provision. Within a short time, I was employed by Boeing and again experiencing God's blessing in my vocation.

Parents, we must teach our children to love and fear the Lord. He will do whatever He must do to lovingly correct His children.

## No Worry

There is much wasted anxiety over one's income. Jesus said, "Therefore I say unto you, Take no thought for your life, what ye shall eat, or what ye shall drink; nor yet for your body, what ye shall put on" (Matthew 6:25). "Take no thought" means do not be anxious or worry about it.

We are not to worry about how much income our sons can earn for their families. However, as we build the foundation of our sons' futures, we need to "count the cost" and consider that there are many important things we need to teach and train them in. If they are pleasing to the Lord, He will provide them with the income that is right for them.

## Questions

1. What is your view of work? What impact do you believe that will have on your son's view of work? Discuss this with your son if he is at an appropriate age.

2. Do you believe a man's view of work will impact his earning potential? Why or why not?

3. Make a list of the positive character traits that a son needs in order to provide for his future family.

4. Make a list of the negative character traits that will hinder a son's ability to support his family.

5. What is your attitude toward new learning opportunities? How does your attitude affect your son's attitude toward learning? Discuss this with your son if he is at an appropriate age.

6. Recall how God has blessed you, personally, through your work. Share this testimony with your son.

7. Has God ever used your job or finances to discipline you? Think back on what happened and what you learned through it. Share this with your son if he is at an age to understand.

———————————

If God says it is good to work, it is. If
God says it is enjoyable and a pleasure
and a reward to work, it is. If we need
to change the way we think and speak
about work, we should. We definitely
are warned not to call that which is
good evil (Isaiah 5:20), and we must
learn to do this with work.
*David Barton*

———————————

# What Does It Take to Make Ends Meet?

---

*There is nothing better for a man, than that*
*he should eat and drink, and that he should*
*make his soul enjoy good in his labour.*
Ecclesiastes 2:24

---

A while ago we were at a gas station, and Mary, who was four years old at the time, held up a penny. She wanted to buy some candy. The only problem was the candy cost fifty cents! She didn't understand that she had to have enough money in hand to purchase an item she wanted. There are many adults who don't understand that same concept!

I know a young wife, Beth, who acquired a taste for nice jewelry. Tommy, her husband, loves her very much and wants to please her. Guess what Tommy buys Beth? Jewelry—beautiful, expensive jewelry. Even though Tommy earns a good income, it isn't sufficient to support extravagant purchases. This couple has chosen to rely on credit cards to feed Beth's jewelry appetite, and they have amassed thousands of dollars of high-interest debt.

How many times have we heard our children or maybe even ourselves say, "I need that!" Unfortunately, often it isn't a real need at all, but only a want. It would be very "profitable" to examine which factors truly determine our spending. Then, equipped with that knowledge, we can incorporate it into the training of our children and significantly impact our son's ability to provide for his family.

## Needs

Christians are bound to God's Word as the standard for their lives. As such, we remember how God has said He considers that we have only two needs—food and clothing (Matthew 6:30). We must look at all other purchases in light of that. It doesn't mean we can't spend money on other things; however, we must exercise caution when we do so. We are assured that our Father will provide our food and clothing (Matthew 6:30). If we spend what He has given us on frivolous things, we may not be given more. Then we will have a problem!

Clearly in our modern era, we would say we have "need" of housing as well. Even though the Lord doesn't call it a need, we can have confidence that He will not ignore it. We read, "If ye then, being evil, know how to give good gifts unto your children, how much more shall your Father which is in heaven give good things to them that ask him?" (Matthew 7:11). We can have confidence in bringing other requests to the Lord.

1 John 5:14 says, "And this is the confidence that we have in him, that, if we ask any thing according to his will, he heareth us." This verse gives us confidence and a caution. We can have confidence in bringing a need for housing before our heavenly Father knowing He will listen and respond. However, the caution is that we can't assume the Lord is going to do whatever we ask. The big question becomes, "Is our request according to His will?"

It is one thing to say, "I want this house or this car." However, it is an entirely different matter to be able to say, "God, I believe purchasing this automobile is Your will for my family." Unless one is superficial in their walk with the Lord, such a statement cannot be said casually. It must be said with an understanding of His Word, after having brought the request to Him in prayer. Real prayer has a way of sifting out the chaff from the wheat.

A son must be able to be content whether God is providing lavishly or sparingly. We can see that Paul understood contentment from Philippians 4:11, "Not that I speak in respect of want: for I have learned, in whatsoever state I am, *therewith* to be content."

In regards to housing, our sons should understand God's view of debt. Paul says in Romans 13:8, "Owe no man any thing, but to love one another: for he that loveth another hath fulfilled the law." If they choose to obtain a mortgage, it would be wise to be done with great caution and the commitment to pay it off as soon as possible. The lust of the flesh sets a trap that many fall into. Often God blesses an individual with a good income. Then he will buy as expensive a house as his income permits. The world calls that a wise thing to do because he is "leveraging" his income.

Herb, from Chapter One, fell for that bait. He is paying on a $750,000 mortgage that is bringing no little pain into his life. That mortgage represents over $6,000 a month in payments alone, without including upkeep and utilities. He now sees the foolishness of buying such an expensive house and desperately wants to sell it, but with no success yet. His 20/20 hindsight tells him he made a mistake. He now understands that just because he had the income to make the payment at one point, that did not mean he could always do so. It is critical that our children learn not to base future spending commitments on the income they are currently receiving. It is good not to presume upon the future: "Boast not thyself of to morrow; for thou knowest not what a day may bring forth" (Proverbs 27:1).

## Size of Family and Residence Location

As we look at a family's needs, it becomes obvious that these needs will be mostly driven by the size of the family and where they live. The more children we have, the greater our need for food and clothing. God may choose to supply those needs in many ways; not all provision comes through a paycheck. As we were beginning our business, the Lord led one sweet woman to give us the clothes her son outgrew. My younger sons were delighted with the very nice clothing they were receiving. Over the last twenty-five years God has regularly chosen to meet our needs through others. There were times when our clothing purchases were practically zero.

It is exciting to see God provide in ways other than a paycheck, and we want to train our children to look to God's hand. It then becomes second nature for them to ask their heavenly Father to meet their needs and to know He provides. Sometimes this means learning to wait instead of running out and buying right away.

In addition to the number of children God has given a family, the area where they choose to live will also greatly affect the amount they spend. By choosing to live in rural Arkansas or downtown New York City, your son will be directly impacting what he spends on his family's needs. It is possible to be frugal in both locations and lower what is spent, but the bottom line will vary significantly between the two. As costly and painful as it may be, ministries and companies will even move their headquarters to a new location to minimize the cost of living.

I have often heard a dad say there is nothing further he can do to lower his family's expenses. However, what he means is, there is nothing more he wants to do to cut expenses. Any additional cuts would affect their standard of living and would not be acceptable. Christian families must be committed to living within God's provision even if it involves simpler living.

The size of our family and where we live are primarily what we think about as the factors that determine how much we spend. However, let's continue to look at four more areas that are even more important.

## Character

Here is where character really pays dividends. Not only will a man of good character spend far less than a man of poor character, your daughter-in-law will also call you blessed for raising such a wonderful husband.

To better illustrate the impact character has on spending, we will list the negative traits as they more clearly illustrate the point.

Lazy—He will expect others to do his work for him. Odd jobs around the home will be hired out to those who are willing to mow the lawn, rake the leaves, shovel snow, and perform household maintenance for a fee.

Fainthearted—He will give up on a project or not even begin one because it seems too hard. Then he will have to pay someone else to do what he could have done.

Procrastinator—He just can't get around to taking care of projects while they are small and manageable. He kept meaning to change the furnace air filter. Now it is too late, and an expensive repair is necessary.

Faithless—He does not believe in God's faithfulness to provide for his family's needs.

Impatient—He will not wait on God but uses credit or funds God intended to be used for other things. Therefore, he buys what he wants when he wants it.

You can see how the list could continue illustrating the manner in which lack of character drastically impacts a man's spending. The man who is industrious, resourceful, orderly, and responsible will need a smaller wallet than one who isn't. Parents have a marvelous opportunity to directly impact their children's future spending simply by training them to be mighty in character.

After Christopher bought his first car at age nineteen, he decided there were several preventative maintenance tasks he should perform. Even though he had no car-related experience, he chose to do the work himself, since none of the jobs required special tools. At one point while changing the transmission fluid and filter, he encountered a very significant problem. With a little encouragement from Dad, he continued to work and pray until he finally succeeded. It was a marvelous lesson in the benefits of determination. Our children's training is not complete until they are men of character.

## Bad Appetites

Remember Jerry in Chapter Three who illustrated someone with a poor view of work? Unfortunately, he is also a great example of someone with negative appetites. I have never known anyone with such incredible passions. He spent every cent he could get his hands on for rifles, pistols, cameras, metal working machines, and amateur radio equipment. I expect he had more interests, but these were primary. Even when he wasn't spending money on them, he was spending his time. Jerry was not a Christian and therefore was not accountable to God for how he spent his time and money. However, for a Christian there is no such thing as idle time or frivolous money.

When I was quite young, my dad used to ask me to get him a "beverage" out of the refrigerator. He would offer me a sip, and

I acquired a taste for it. Is it a wonder that as a teenager, prior to being saved, I enjoyed drinking? Think about what an expensive and damaging appetite that could have grown into.

Appetites when fed become passions. Parents need to be extremely careful about which appetites they create in their children. We will have more to say about good and bad appetites later on.

## God's Hand of Discipline

I have had friends share that extra expenses were burying them. As the discussions progress, I discover they aren't tithing. In Malachi 2:2 God said He would curse blessings. Then we go on to read in Chapter 3, verses 8 and 9, "Will a man rob God? Yet ye have robbed me. But ye say, Wherein have we robbed thee? In tithes and offerings. Ye *are* cursed with a curse: for ye have robbed me, *even* this whole nation" (Malachi 3:8-9). This is pretty clear that there is a curse on those who choose not to honor God with their tithes. Wouldn't it make sense for God to punish a man financially because he was refusing to honor God with his finances?

Scripture also has other warnings that a man is wise to heed. "A prudent *man* foreseeth the evil, and hideth himself: but the simple pass on, and are punished" (Proverbs 22:3). A son will be well prepared if he knows and obeys the warnings of Scripture. An excellent way to teach the family the wisdom and cautions of Proverbs would be to read the chapter in Proverbs that corresponds with the day of the month. Then discuss which verse each person found to have special meaning to them. It will have a powerful effect on their lives.

Therefore, it is imperative that we teach our children to love the Lord Jesus and live pleasing to Him. Otherwise, their loving Father in heaven will discipline them when it is needed (Hebrews 12:6-7).

## Spouse

Parents can do a wonderful job of raising their children and still end up with a son who can't provide for his family. How can that be? "Therefore shall a man leave his father and his mother, and shall cleave unto his wife: and they shall be one flesh" (Genesis 2:24). When a man takes a wife, they become one.

Remember Tommy, whose wife loved expensive jewelry? That is what can happen if our sons take wives who haven't had similar training. The spouse's shortcomings will affect the marriage as a whole. If the wife is not content, she will want a bigger house, nicer furniture, or the most fashionable clothes. If she isn't a diligent worker she will want to eat out often, buy the latest work-saving gadget, and hire someone to help with things that she could do herself. All of the factors that affect spending for the son apply to the wife as well. Her spending habits will be directly related to the training she has received.

## The Parents' Responsibility

Our sons need to learn what factors affect their spending and how they have direct control over most of them. They are not helpless victims of life but are to be obedient men of God.

As parents, we see the tremendous opportunity we have to influence our sons in these areas that will impact their "real" earning potential. We will teach our sons these principles during the years they are children living in our homes through purposeful discussions. We should look for opportunities to model our own contentedness and positive character. Sharing with our sons our own character failures and the consequences the family has suffered as a result will be a powerful teaching tool in the hand of a father.

In addition, we never want to lose sight of the necessity of prayer, first for our own lives in each of these areas, and then for our sons.

## Questions

1. Define the difference between a need and a want.

2. Do you pray before you make a purchase?

3. Have you taught your children to pray about purchases by including them in praying for items your family needs?

4. How have you learned, in your life, to be content? Discuss with your son the specific situations the Lord has used to teach you contentment.

5. How does your location affect your ability to provide for your family?

6. Can you relate to any of the negative character traits discussed in this chapter? If so, how have they affected your ability to provide for your family?

7. Can you think of appetites in your life that have caused you to waste family finances? What are they?

8. Are you tithing? If not, will you make a commitment to begin to do so?

9. Have you studied Proverbs to discover the warnings there? Begin teaching your sons from Proverbs on whatever level they can understand.

10. How does your wife help or hinder in making ends meet? Praise her for her help and encourage her in her areas of weakness.

———————————

A man who gives his children habits of industry provides for them better than by giving them a fortune.
*Whately*

We endeavor to "Train up a child in the way
he should go" (Proverbs 22:6) by instilling in
them during their earliest years the very
foundations they will need for success
throughout the remainder of their life.
*David Barton*

———————————

# Three Pillars of Training Sons

---

*And also that every man should eat and drink, and
enjoy the good of all his labour, it is the gift of God.*
Ecclesiastes 3:13

---

You will find that the thrust of this book can be condensed
into a three-legged stool analogy. Consider a three-legged stool. It
never wobbles if one leg is a little shorter than the others as the legs
compensate for each other by design. However, if one leg is significantly shorter, we will not expect long-term satisfaction from
the stool.

To prepare a son to provide for a one-income family, you will
need three key components: your training, your example, and
your prayer. We must not get lazy and neglect any one area by
assuming it won't matter, because it does. Almost every aspect of
this book refers back to one of these three key elements.

## Teaching Versus Training

As parents it is easy to be shortsighted regarding the preparation that is required in a child's life to produce a responsible adult.
The definition of the word "teach" focuses on imparting knowledge. We all know how hard that can be. No doubt homeschooling moms will echo, "Amen!" Training, on the other hand, is even
more difficult to accomplish and far more important than simply

focusing on drills, repetition, and correction. Training affects the behavior of the one being trained as opposed to the simple accumulation of facts.

Let me illustrate this by example. Teri, my wife, may teach our twelve-year-old son that the trash is to be taken out three times a day to maintain an orderly kitchen. Our son may understand and know this mentally. Unfortunately, that doesn't mean he is going to take the trash out!

Teri begins training by first showing him what is expected and how to do it. Then she helps him associate the job with a specific time, such as just prior to sitting down at the table to eat. After this our twelve-year-old knows what he is responsible to do, how to do it from demonstration and practice, and finally its association with an event to help him remember. After all of that, Teri may use daily inspections, rewards, or consequences to ensure he stays motivated until emptying the trash becomes a consistent behavior for our son. Doesn't training sound like a lot more work than teaching?

## The Least Understood Verse

While preparing for a workshop, I recently came to a new understanding of the well-known verse, "Train up a child in the way he should go, and when he is old, he will not depart from it" (Proverbs 22:6). I believe this is one of the most quoted verses in family-related, Christian forums. However, it is also misunderstood and thereby inappropriately applied. We must grasp the meaning of Proverbs 22:6 and apply it correctly if we want to reap its benefits.

How could a verse that seems so straightforward be misapplied? Does it teach us that if we raise our children in the way we want them to live, they will continue to live that way when they are adults? Through many years I have observed "good" Christian parents raising their children—families who attend church, espouse to love the Lord Jesus, and even homeschool their children. Are they training these children in the way they should go, and will the seedling adults become diligent workers and dedicated Christians?

## What Does It Really Mean?

Since Scripture instructs us to "Train up a child in the way he should go and when he is old he will not depart," let's take a few minutes to examine these words. First observe that "train up" is the Hebrew word "chanak." The expanded meaning of this word is "start" or "inaugurate." In the four other places it is used, it refers to structures that were built. This is appropriate since child training is a process that must have a purposed beginning point, and it takes effort expended in accordance with a plan. If you are building and aren't working according to a quality plan, you cannot have confidence that your efforts will result in anything worthwhile.

The word "chanak" is in the imperative tense. That means it is a command to be obeyed. God did not say we should think about this and come to a decision. Simply put, we must do it.

The phrase "in the way he should go" raises the question, how do we know "which way" he is to go? Is it to be in the way the parents want him to go? Is the child the parent's opportunity to live out their unfulfilled expectations? Perhaps the father who always wanted to star in sports can now groom and coach his son to be that star. Maybe Dad wanted to be a doctor and never had the opportunity.

I believe we find the answer to "which way" by looking at two more verses. First in Malachi 2:15 we read, "And did not he make one? Yet had he the residue of the spirit. And wherefore one? That he might seek a godly seed." God's purpose for marriage was to result in godly offspring. That means children are to be dedicated each day of their lives to God Almighty and His plan for their lives. "Which way" isn't the way the parents think the child should live, but it is to be in accordance with God's direction for that child.

Second we read, "Before I formed thee in the belly I knew thee; and before thou camest forth out of the womb I sanctified thee, *and* I ordained thee a prophet unto the nations" (Jeremiah 1:5). God has a plan for each child, and it will be consistent with His Word. We must lay down our agendas in favor of the direction the Lord has for him.

"When he is old" is translated from the Hebrew word that is used when the Old Testament speaks of elders. It was used to describe Abraham, Sarah, Samuel, Saul, and others when they had become aged.

"He will not depart" means he will not be removed from the path. Rather the path will be a friend to him. He will not feel comfortable leaving it for long. He will not forsake the godly way of life in which he has been trained. However, as he journeys through life he is still in the flesh. He will stumble and sin just like we do, but sin will not be his master. In his desire to live a life pleasing to the Lord Jesus and to his parents, he will not be at peace when walking in sin and will repent.

We can now verbosely restate the verse as "Begin the process of building up your child in accordance with God's Word and His specific blueprint for your child's life. When he is old, he will continue to live that way." Friends, I find great comfort in that! Sadly, this verse is frequently used to comfort parents who have not raised children according to God's plan and whose children are now in rebellion. Those using Proverbs 22:6 in this way are implying that the verse means the child will eventually be a dedicated man of God because he was brought to church several times a week. That just isn't true!

## The Misunderstanding

This is why I say Proverbs 22:6 is the most misunderstood verse. Parents seem to believe they can raise their children any way they want and those children will still turn out to be pleasing to God. This seems to be especially true of families who attend church and lead "moral" lives.

I'm seeing children who are being raised to be children all of their lives. They are being trained, but not in the way they should go. It appears that either parents do not have Scriptural goals for their children, or they are not raising their children consistent with their goals. The result will be the same. Parents need to ask themselves what their goals are for their children. They then should examine those goals to see if they are consistent with Scripture. In another twenty years, the entertainment-focused Christian youth of today will be entertainment-focused adults who act much like they did in their teen years. It was true of my generation, and I'm confident it will be true for this current one also.

If the years of one's youth mean one fun activity or sport after another, when do children learn to enjoy work? Must our children always have great fun while being educated? Will it spoil their childhood if they don't have lots of playtime? Am I more concerned that my child will shake his finger in my face and whine, "You deprived me of being a child!" or of him not being a man of God who is able to provide adequately for a family? "But if any provide not for his own, and specially for those of his own house, he hath denied the faith, and is worse than an infidel" (1 Timothy 5:8).

How will our children, when they are adults, respond to jobs that aren't always fun? In my last corporate job, my title was Procurement Engineer; I was hired to do product investigations and research. However, after a few years in this job, I began to regularly have to ship small quantities of sample items to another division. Because there was no way the shipping department could charge my department back for materials, shipping, and time, I had to do all the shipping myself. Packaging the items and filling out customs and shipping paperwork were not found anywhere in my job description! Some of my coworkers even thought I was crazy for doing it. They said that someone else should have to do that shipping. I would have been grateful had the billing issue been resolved. Then someone in shipping would have taken over this part of my responsibility, but for the longest time I needed to do it. I wasn't excited about it, but since it had to be done, I was willing.

I expect many of you could give examples of jobs you are required to do that are not "fun." It is life and a part of being a mature worker. Christians are called to work, and work by definition refers to an activity requiring effort. Our world has come to the conclusion that expending effort for anything work-related is not a pleasurable experience. It does not matter whether it is physical exertion or mental, it still is to be avoided. What is amazing is that laziness and ignorance are glamorized in the media. From my observation of many teens, the media has succeeded in making slothfulness "cool" and desirable.

The essence of Proverbs 22:6 is that we reap what we sow. That is what Galatians 6:7-8 says, "Be not deceived; God is not mocked: for whatsoever a man soweth, that shall he also reap. For he that soweth to his flesh shall of the flesh reap corruption; but he that soweth to the Spirit shall of the Spirit reap life everlasting."

We need to train our children according to God's Word and His direction, expecting it to be hard work. It is critical that we keep our hand to the plow, never slacking as we endeavor to raise up a godly generation. Then as the days, weeks, months, and years go by our young men will grow up to provide for their families and be equipped to train their children.

## Our Example

The next pillar that we will examine is the parent's example. You, as a parent, play a pivotal role in the maturing process of your sons.

My family knows that I am consistent about my daily, private Bible reading and prayer time. During my weekly meetings with my older children, I will often ask them about their devotions. I'm delighted that they all take the necessity of having their own quiet time very seriously. If spending time alone with the Lord were not a daily part of my life, it would have been far more difficult to encourage my children to do so.

One personal shortcoming of mine, and I wish there were fewer, is lack of orderliness. I am willing to tolerate messiness in areas that are my responsibility. I desire to change this by giving it my needed time and attention.

Teri, on the other hand, is very orderly. Do you want to guess which example our children follow? Mine! Most children are disorderly by nature, and having a parent struggle in the same way only reinforces those tendencies. As a result of my example, additional time and effort must go into training our children to be orderly. While it is possible to train a child to a higher character level than his parent, it is not easy!

Pick any bad habit a father might have and some form of it will often be impressed on the children. I wish it weren't like that, but seeing my sin in my children's lives is a giant stimulus for me to change my ways. "For whom he did foreknow, he also did predestinate *to be* conformed to the image of his Son" (Romans 8:29). We need to be zealous that our life is pleasing to the Lord so our example is one of godly encouragement.

## Prayer

The third aspect of raising a godly son who is able to provide for his family is often ignored or only given token attention. Let me introduce this third aspect through a family anecdote.

Christopher, my second-born son, is extremely talented. Unfortunately, abilities also make it easy to become proud. When Christopher was twenty-one years old, we saw him exhibit increasingly prideful attitudes. My heart was concerned. I discussed this with him over a period of time during our weekly one-on-one meetings. In addition to speaking with Christopher about his pride, I had been praying that God would work in his life.

One day Christopher suddenly developed severe pain in first one wrist and soon after in the other one as well. He could no longer do the things that fueled his pride—piano playing, graphic design, and photography. Literally overnight, the very things Christopher depended on for his livelihood and pleasure were gone. We had a teachable moment!

He had heeded me during our weekly meetings and desired to change, but now his heart was listening as well. I shared with him that I believed the wrist pain was primarily a spiritual issue and secondarily a medical one. I suggested he cry out to the Lord in prayer and fasting, asking God to change his heart. As Christopher began to pray, he felt God leading him to a fast that he continued five days. During that fasting time we all noticed a wonderful change. In fact, one evening while we were having family altar, even the younger children commented on the change they were seeing in Christopher and how much they liked it. He was truly a changed man.

My encouragement was to pray for God's will to be done in his life. If his talent was going to fuel his pride, it would be better to do without those things in his life (Matthew 5:29-30).

This story highlights the third aspect of child training—prayer. "Praying always with all prayer and supplication in the Spirit, and watching thereunto with all perseverance and supplication for all saints" (Ephesians 6:18). We have seen God work in our children's hearts many times through the years and how critical prayer is for direction in our child rearing.

Friends, I am not sure about you, but I do not have confidence in my ability to be a perfect example and teach my sons everything they need to know to be men of God, rightfully leading and providing for their family. I am committed to doing my best, but I do not have confidence in the "flesh." Therefore, I must cry out for God to work in my children's hearts. The quantity of time I pray for my children represents my humility and dependence on my Father in Heaven.

In Luke 18:1-8 Jesus uses a widow and an unjust judge as our encouragement to pray fervently. He is not teaching us that we are "twisting God's arm" through persistent prayers. We are clearly told to pray, especially for God's will. Jesus uses this parable as an example that we are to pray fervently, and that is what I'm going to do. If God can change the heart of an ungodly, unjust, and wicked judge, He can surely work in the hearts of our children.

God provided Christopher as an excellent example at the perfect point in writing this book. We would have preferred that situations are always perfect in the Maxwell home, but that isn't the case. We are sinners saved by grace, and not one of us has "arrived." But praise God: He is merciful and not slack in giving us grace. Yes, God truly hears and answers prayers.

By looking at how God equips us for the task of raising godly seed, we should be filled with gratitude. If we had to depend solely on our own example and our training abilities, we might be discouraged at times. However, praise God that He also works in hearts and answers prayer. Remember that He wants godly seed even more than we do.

## Three-Legged Stool

As we continue to discuss how to train sons to provide for a single-income family, you will often see parts of the three-legged stool analogy. It is imperative that we train our sons in the skills and character they will need to equip them for life. Along with this training, we must be the positive example to our sons of everything we would like to see develop in them. Without our example, they may view all our training as hypocritical. Lastly, we rely on the third leg of that stool, prayer. No matter how much we train and how great our example, the Lord is the One Who will ultimately train and equip each son. May we not neglect our dependence on prayer for the Lord's work in every son's life.

## Questions

1. Reflect on how Proverbs 22:6 has been explained. Has this changed your understanding of the verse? If so, what might you now do differently in raising your children?

2. What does the Bible say about the way in which you train your children?

3. What is the difference between teaching and training? If you don't know, look it up in the dictionary. Have you been teaching or training your children?

4. Are there inconsistencies in what you want as the outcome for your child versus how you are training him? Think of fun-focused or work-focused training, for example.

5. Were you taught or trained as a child? How has that affected your life?

6. Is your example such that the Lord is pleased?

7. Would you be pleased if your son became a perfect copy of you?

8. What would you like to change in your example?

9. How often are you praying for specific needs in your children's lives?

10. How often are you praying for specific direction in your child rearing?

---

Consider the Biblical case for honoring (and thus
teaching children to honor) work. In Exodus 20:9,
God declares, "Six days shalt thou labour, and do all
thy work." Notice He did not say, "Six days 'may' you
work"; He said "shalt." In fact, God Himself set us
the example. In Exodus 20:11, God tells us that He
worked for six days, and then rested.

*David Barton*

---

# How Sure a Foundation?

---

*Six days shalt thou labour, and do all thy work.*
*Exodus 20:9*

---

There is little doubt that the architect and builders of *La Torre de Pisa* would have been thrilled to have their bell tower masterpiece so well known throughout the world. However, would they have been as thrilled if most of the attention were due to a defect and not the exquisite architecture? The Leaning Tower of Pisa is an architectural marvel, however a sure foundation is certainly lacking.

A son that truly is a child of the King and is about the Master's business will have confidence that his Lord will provide for all of his needs. "But seek ye first the kingdom of God, and his righteousness; and all these things shall be added unto you" (Matthew 6:33). That son is looking to the Lord Jesus for direction in his day-to-day affairs, and dear parent, you can have peace that he is in good Hands and will be taken care of.

Let us now look at a number of foundational factors that are critical for our lives so we will be good examples for our children. These also must become part of our children's lives. We should live them and teach them, and our sons have to receive them into their lives. So what are they?

## Salvation

Nathan, my oldest son, worked with Mike for a number of months. Mike is single, good looking, extremely talented, and makes an enormous amount of money. He lives the "fast life," drives high performance German vehicles, and goes from one fun experience to another. Do Mike's parents consider him a success? Very likely! Most people evaluate their children's success by the amount of money they earn and whether they stay out of trouble. Unfortunately, Mike doesn't know the Lord Jesus as Savior, and unless something changes, he will spend eternity in "the lake of fire."

"For what is a man profited, if he shall gain the whole world, and lose his own soul? or what shall a man give in exchange for his soul?" (Matthew 16:26). What good is it to raise a son who can provide luxuriously for a family and yet does not know the Lord Jesus? If that is the case, we have failed as parents.

For us to set the right example, we must ask ourselves if we are saved. It is not a matter of being religious, but are we saved? Do we have a real relationship with the Lord Jesus Christ? Of the various cast members I've mentioned, some appeared to be saved, some might have had a walk with Christ that was distant - there was little fruit in their lives - and a few were likely lost. At best, religion may change a man's outward behavior, but Jesus Christ changes a man's heart and will save him from eternity in hell.

Without a real relationship with Jesus Christ, we are vastly limited in our ability to prepare our children and lead our family. One reason the United States military has been very successful is because of the technology they use in communications and reconnaissance. Ask an infantryman how important a forward observer or a spotter aircraft is to him in avoiding areas of great danger. Ask an airman how important radar is in evading hostile ships and aircraft. Ask a sailor how important his GPS (Global Positioning System) receiver is in determining how to get where he needs to go.

Without the Lord, we might as well be in a bottle on the high seas, carried about by the ocean currents and wind. When we have the Spirit of the living God indwelling us, we have real purpose in life and limitless resources available if we will but use them.

When we are not saved, life on earth is all we have to look forward to. Our few years here are as good as it gets, and it is no wonder that the lost live for every ounce of pleasure they can purchase. However, those who have been bought by the blood of the Lord Jesus ought not to live like that. Our possessions will come to nothing, but our children will live on.

Which is more important—our children's salvation or "things"? Is the salvation of our children a burning desire on our hearts? It probably won't be if we aren't saved ourselves. "And this is his commandment, That we should believe on the name of his Son Jesus Christ, and love one another, as he gave us commandment" (1 John 3:23).

So what does it mean to be saved? Is "saved" an archaic term from years gone by with no relevance for our day? Certainly not! "Saved" means we enter into a dynamic relationship with God the Father through the blood of Jesus Christ. It means that we are guilty sinners standing before a righteous and holy God, fully accepting the fact that Jesus died on the cross to pay for our personal sins. It means we believe that on the third day Jesus rose from the dead and is now seated at the right hand of God. It means we believe we will spend eternity with Him in Heaven. It means we are willing to give total control of every aspect of our lives to Jesus. Salvation must be a personal experience between you and the Lord Jesus. Here is how:

1. Realize you are a sinner before a holy God. "For all have sinned, and come short of the glory of God" (Romans 3:23). "All" means "all," and we can't be saved unless we see our death sentence due to our sin. That seems to be a stumbling

block for the religious. They don't view themselves as sinners. The Bible says salvation is not a matter of being better than others or having done more good deeds than others, the question is whether we have ever broken God's law. "For whosoever shall keep the whole law, and yet offend in one *point*, he is guilty of all" (James 2:10). If we have ever stolen, coveted, lied, or dishonored our parents, we are sinners before a holy God.

2. Repent means to change the course of our thinking. No longer are we satisfied to live for ourselves, but we desire to let God have control over our lives. "I tell you, Nay: but, except ye repent, ye shall all likewise perish" (Luke 13:3).

3. Receive Jesus. The purpose of Christ dying on the cross was to take the penalty of our sins on Himself. The sinless died for the sinner, the innocent traded His life for the condemned. "But as many as received him, to them gave he power to become the sons of God, *even* to them that believe on his name" (John 1:12).

4. Rejoice in the fact that you are now born again. "Which were born, not of blood, nor of the will of the flesh, nor of the will of man, but of God" (John 1:13). As God is your witness, if you meant it, you have been saved.

5. Recount publicly what God has done for you. "That if thou shalt confess with thy mouth the Lord Jesus, and shalt believe in thine heart that God hath raised him from the dead, thou shalt be saved. For with the heart man believeth unto righteousness; and with the mouth confession is made unto salvation" (Romans 10:9-10). Tell others that you have been saved and that you are now a Christian.

## Personal Quiet Time

David is a Christian and told me about a difficult decision he was facing. He had an attractive job offer in another city with significantly higher pay and better working conditions. He was praying about whether to accept it. Unfortunately, it would mean moving his family away from extended family, friends, and the church that they loved. It was such a wonderful opportunity, and he was interested in my counsel.

I asked him how the Lord was directing him, and he said he couldn't discern. I began to probe into his relationship with the Lord Jesus and the quality of his quiet times (personal Bible reading and prayer). As our discussion progressed it became obvious that time with the Lord Jesus wasn't a priority, and it was only after this job offer that he sought time with his Lord.

To put this in perspective, let's use a more personal example that every married person should be able to understand. Remember Kevin from Chapter One? He would get into disagreements with his wife if they spent too much time together. In essence, their marriage was nothing more than a convenient arrangement of shared responsibilities that enabled them to pursue their own separate interests. If there had been intimacy of heart in their relationship, they would have longed to spend time together.

There was a time when Teri and I noticed our relationship was suffering. We disagreed easily and didn't enjoy time together. A situation arose that required us to spend a long day together away from home.

A very interesting thing happened as the day progressed. We found the sweetness of our relationship was being restored. Our discussions were no longer labored and testy, but pleasant. We enjoyed being together and became best friends again.

To promote intimacy in any relationship, there is no substitute for spending time together. The question is, "Do you want to be close to your Lord and to be able to hear His direction for your life?" If so, I'm convinced there is no better way than by having a quality quiet time each morning.

Let's go back to David and his job offer. His relationship with the Lord Jesus was not intimate. As a result, he was unable to hear what the Lord was telling him about the job. In fact, not having a quiet time is probably what allowed him to be attracted to another job in the first place. He was willing to sacrifice his family's peace because of his discontent with his job. Had he been taking the struggles he was having with his current job to the Lord, the situation would likely have been resolved without his needing to run away.

In fact, I have observed this to be a common occurrence in families. The Lord wants to work in the father's life through some job challenges. Instead of humbling himself, the dad reacts, and the situation worsens. Soon a new job is seen as his only option. We must be willing to let God use the uncomfortable situations of daily life to conform us to the image of His Son. "For whom he did foreknow, he also did predestinate *to be* conformed to the image of his Son" (Romans 8:29).

Can you now see how a daily, undisturbed time with the Lord Jesus is critical to spiritual health? Without it our relationship with Him becomes malnourished, weakened, and one of mere outward religious conformity. There is no joy in such a Christian walk, and there is certainly nothing our children would want to adopt for their life. One reason so many parents lose their children to the world is because the children observe their parents' hypocritical religious walk and want nothing to do with it. To maintain a sweet walk with the Savior we must spend time with Him. Then we can effectively encourage and train our children in the discipline of a daily quiet time as well.

Children must see their parents depending on quiet time with the Lord for daily direction. They should want that for themselves. They need to know that Jesus Christ will provide direction for their lives if they will maintain fellowship with Him. They have to realize their daily quiet time is the primary way of enriching their walk with their Savior.

I believe that when I have discipled my children to the point where they are looking to their Lord for direction, my job is finished. That doesn't mean they will never ask my counsel or that I won't give it. However, while I'm still on this earth, I am at peace knowing they are seeking first and foremost the Lord's guidance. Think about it. If our children are looking intently at their Lord for direction and they have developed the sensitivity needed to follow His leading, they should never make a bad decision. How could we improve on that?

Now that we understand how imperative a daily, individual time with the Lord is, you might be interested in some quiet-time mechanics.

## When?

Whatever task is most important in my day, I do first. That is why I must have my time with the Lord Jesus right after I rise in the morning. Otherwise it either won't happen, or it will be superficial at best. Before the telephone starts ringing and other distractions begin screaming for attention, I have my time with the Lord.

I have heard dads tell me they don't have time for their Bible reading before work. After further discussion, I have yet to see it be true for any of them. If they viewed their devotion as the life's blood of their walk with the Lord, they would do whatever it took to spend time with Him.

When a couple is falling in love, will they let other "things" get in the way of their spending time together? No! We will make time for what is important to us. That is worth repeating! We WILL make time for what is important to us. If we are not daily spending time with the Lord, let us be mature and admit it really isn't important to us. Then at least our families won't consider us hypocrites.

## Where?

I go to my office that is located in the corner of the basement to read my Bible and pray. Early in the morning the office is quiet. I am more likely to be consistent if I use the same location each day. The Bible I use for my devotions is always on the shelf beside my desk so I don't have to hunt for it.

I have known a couple men who were so limited in house space they actually used a lighted closet for their quiet times. Not only was it effective, but Scriptural. "But thou, when thou prayest, enter into thy closet, and when thou hast shut thy door, pray to thy Father which is in secret; and thy Father which seeth in secret shall reward thee openly" (Matthew 6:6).

There is always someplace we can go to be alone. When on our family vacation and staying in a small cabin, I hiked up the side of the mountain to be alone with my Lord. It was wonderful. If you can't find a private place, then cry out to the Lord in prayer. He wants to spend time with you, and He will show you where.

## What?

I read the Bible and would wholeheartedly encourage you to do the same. I know there are many devotionals available that make reading enjoyable by providing a short Scripture, a touching anecdote, and a nice warm feeling. However, why settle for what someone else thinks you should read? Why not depend on the Lord? We need to hear directly from the Lord. May we always want God's best and not settle for second best.

I try to be sensitive to where, in the Bible, the Lord wants me to read. There are some years when I read through the Bible, and other times when I focus on a particular section of Scripture. Not too long ago, He led me to read, over and over, the four gospels: Matthew, Mark, Luke, and John. When it was time to stop that, the Lord directed me to read Genesis, Exodus, and Joshua for quite some time. Lately, He has had me reading the writings of Peter and John. If you don't know where in the Bible to begin reading, start in the New Testament or the book of John.

It is always exciting to see how the Lord leads me to passages of Scripture in my daily quiet times that directly apply to situations we are experiencing. Recently our children were having some difficulties suffering what they considered injustices perpetrated upon them by their siblings. I realized that 1 Peter had much to say about suffering because I had been reading it in my devotions. We then began reading 1 Peter during our family altar time. The insights I had gained from my time with the Lord prepared me to share, challenge, and encourage during our family devotions. Do we want to be instruments prepared and ready for the Master's use? If so, let us let Him guide our Bible reading.

## How?

The sequence I use for my quiet times is generally the same. I begin by reading my Bible with an attitude of, "Lord, show me what you have for me today." What current need am I seeking His direction for? I don't have a set number of pages or chapters to read. Some days I may only read a handful of verses that are rich with meaning and teaching. Other days I read several chapters.

After reading my Bible, I go to my Lord in prayer. Prayer is a very special part of my quiet time. I spend up to half of my quiet time praying. As I begin I seek a clear conscience, so I confess, repent, and ask forgiveness for sin that He brings to mind. Next I praise Him for Who He is and how He has blessed us. Then I intercede for others. It may be issues with the children or needs of others. Finally, I will bring to my Lord whatever needs we have.

## Hindrances to Quiet Time

I believe the greatest hindrance to our having a quality, daily quiet time is our pride. The more we realize how dependent we are on our Lord for everything, the more we value our time with Him.

There are many things that will appear to hinder a quiet time, but they are only the surface causes. The root cause is always our pride. If there is time to eat and sleep, there is time to be with our Lord.

## Amen!

When we discovered the house across the street was going up for sale our son Nathan, who was twenty-three at the time, was quite interested. However, since he lived with us and didn't have plans to move out, Nathan had no immediate need of a house. He started to pray about the house during his quiet time with the Lord.

Nathan prayed for a number of weeks and finally had confidence that the Lord was telling him to buy it. Additionally, he was surprised to feel God was also telling him it was time to be married. This may not sound surprising since his age was right, he had a good income, and he was a mature believer. However, Nathan was fully at peace with remaining single until God directed him to seek a spouse. Now it appeared that God was directing.

Nathan told the homeowners that he wanted to buy the house, and they gave him a selling price. There was only one problem. He was about ten thousand dollars short of what they wanted. However, Nathan wasn't troubled about the lack of money because he knew that if the Lord were truly involved, He would provide the finances.

Shortly thereafter, a publisher approached Nathan about writing a book on computer security. It would be used in classrooms where Microsoft Certified Systems Engineer curriculum was being taught. Since the proposed writing schedule was extremely aggressive, it was another issue to take to his Lord. After praying he felt God's leading to accept the job. My heart affirmed his decision.

The conclusion to the story is that not only did Nathan complete the book within the agreed-upon time, but the writing's remuneration provided what was needed for him to purchase the house debt free. That was also the fulfillment of a vision for Teri and me; we have encouraged our sons that one aspect of marriage preparation is that they be able to purchase a house debt free.

I do not believe Nathan could have discerned God's leading if he weren't in the habit of having a daily time with the Lord. A parent's daily time with the Lord is essential for his life and critical to imparting the same discipline in the lives of his children.

## Knowledge of the Bible

I spent four years in the Air Force. One thing was constantly hammered into our heads: "Do it by the book!" "The book" was the Air Force Technical Orders (TO) that covered every aspect of aircraft maintenance. Any time there was a malfunction, you were required to look up the troubleshooting procedures and then follow them step by step until the defective part was found. The TO also told you how to replace the part and verify that the entire system was operational again.

Unfortunately, most Airman I knew disliked using TOs! I think there were primarily two reasons: they were not comfortable using the TOs, and it slowed them down.

I observe some similarities between a Christian's reliance on God's Word and an Airman's on his TO. First, we see that the one in authority is the one who provided written instructions. They are not optional. The only way we become comfortable with them is by using them. If we are going to follow the Bible's teachings we must study the Bible so we will know what it teaches. "Study to shew thyself approved unto God, a workman that needeth not to be ashamed, rightly dividing the word of truth" (2 Timothy 2:15). We should understand the Bible and so must our children if they are to be prepared for life.

God's Word warns us of many traps that have severe consequences. We are to beware of the fool, of co-signing for someone's loan, of being unequally yoked, adultery, stealing, lying, and the list goes on. In the same way, an Airman is saved from potential problems by obeying, to the letter, his TO.

Second, following instructions benefits all concerned. If an Airman does not follow the TO for repairs, he jeopardizes the lives of the entire aircrew. If a father does not know and follow God's

Word, he is putting his family at risk, maybe even the risk of eternal judgment.

There is a difference between the two, and it emphasizes the personal relationship of a walk with the Lord Jesus. The Air Force gave step-by-step instructions because they did not want Airmen running to the authorities with a million questions. Don't bother asking questions because you already have the answer in your TO.

God gave us the Bible with direct application to every situation; often, however, we don't find exact step-by-step instructions. Have you ever wondered why? I believe it is the same reason why Jesus healed people in different ways. One He spoke to, another He touched, and another He sent to wash in a pool. I think He wants us listening to Him and being obedient to His directions. We are prone to religiously following a list of steps that leave Him out of the loop. By giving us the general direction, but few specifics, we are forced to listen to Him.

We must seek His guidance for proper application. He wants us to come to Him constantly. The Lord Jesus is our example, and Jesus constantly looked to the Father for what He should do. "Then answered Jesus and said unto them, Verily, verily, I say unto you, The Son can do nothing of himself, but what he seeth the Father do: for what things soever he doeth, these also doeth the Son likewise" (John 5:19).

"Then said Jesus to them again, Peace *be* unto you: as *my* Father hath sent me, even so send I you" (John 20:21). Jesus sought God's will not only regarding the cross, but in all aspects of His life. In the same way, we should seek Him not just when we have difficult decisions to make, but for all facets of our lives.

Years ago, I tried to encourage Ralph in his walk with the Lord. He had shared with our pastor that he was struggling with his faith and wanted to work things out with help.

At one point in our discussions he said he was homosexual and was praying about whether to divorce his wife. Only God knows whether Ralph was actually saved or not, but one thing is clear: Ralph knew very little about what the Bible said concerning the issues of divorce and homosexuality. Of even greater sadness is that Ralph did not understand God's deep love for him.

With today's study Bibles, Ralph could easily have looked up topics in the index to discover what God had to say about the issues he was wrestling. Ralph's discouragement showed that he was suffering with the consequences of his sin. He was certainly looking for a solution. Unfortunately, he wanted to cling to sin and experience the sweetness of a walk with the Savior at the same time. That will never happen!

Sin is an awful master that exacts a heavy toll from all under its power. Do we know what God's Word says about sin and are we able to teach that to our family? When children think of us, do they have confidence in our ability to rightly divide God's Word? It is easy to teach children when they are young, but as they mature, their questions will be more difficult and their evaluation of our answers more intense. Are we workmen that needeth not be ashamed?

## Memorization and Meditation

A very special part of learning God's Word is memorization. The best way I know to understand a section of Scripture is to memorize and then meditate on it. I begin this process by researching each word and looking up other Bible references relating to the verse. Then I am ready to actually memorize the verses.

After memorization comes meditation. Meditation is not some mystical, cultish activity, but rather slowly going over the verse in your mind. Picture how you lingeringly chew on food you enjoy to appreciate every bit of flavor. Similarly, just when you think you've learned everything possible from a verse, the Holy Spirit will open up new insight and deeper application. It is wonderful to experience the fullness of God's Word.

As the Bible is studied and you discover its riches, it becomes obvious that God is not silent on any subject. The exact English word may not be found in the Bible, but there are precepts and truths to be found that can always be applied. Teaching your sons from your own Biblical base of knowledge will be both rewarding to you and beneficial to them.

## Contentment

When is enough money really enough? Herb earns a tremendous income and yet isn't satisfied. Why is Scott content with a painter's income when his family is twice as large as Herb's? Both are Christians who love the Lord. Clearly one is not content and the other one is.

Your attitude regarding your income is far more important than how much money you actually make. Are you trusting God to meet your needs? If we can't trust God to meet our needs, how can we ever trust Him to save us from hell? Which one is more difficult for Him?

If you feel God isn't providing enough money for your family, what do you base that on? Is it because there isn't enough food to eat or because you can't afford a new car? Could it be possible you misspent what He has already given you? Paul said, "I know both how to be abased, and I know how to abound: everywhere and in all things I am instructed both to be full and to be hungry, both to abound and to suffer need" (Philippians 4:12).

God loved Paul and yet He allowed His apostle to suffer need for a season. Why would we ever assume it would be different for us? God used suffering to teach Paul a lesson that could not have been learned any other way. We read in the next verse, "I can do all things through Christ which strengtheneth me" (Philippians 4:13). Paul learned that he could depend on the Lord for everything!

Parents, are you content with the Lord's provision for your needs? Have you learned you can depend on Him for everything? Are you willing to learn the lessons the Lord wants you to learn through suffering? Fathers, may we faithfully walk according to God's Word and be at peace knowing we are having a positive impact on our sons' lives by our example.

## Stewardship

Have you ever let your son use your tools with instructions as to where they are to be returned, only to find them left in the driveway or yard? This example illustrates the essence of poor stewardship.

A steward can be defined as a manager of another's household, estate, or property. Jesus illustrated the concept of a steward clearly for us in Matthew 25. While the Master is away, He has entrusted certain talents and possessions to us to be used according to His instructions.

Do you consider your possessions, time, money—everything—the Lord's? It isn't a matter of what we want to do with each of these, but rather how He instructs us to use them. Are you careful to set the example for your sons by putting your tools away when you are finished with them? Do you ask the Lord whether you should spend the money He has given you to purchase a particular item?

Modeling and teaching good stewardship starts with the practices your children observe in Dad and Mom. Stewardship will help your children learn to wisely use what the Lord has entrusted to them and also to care for it properly.

## Hungry Soul

"Blessed *are* they which do hunger and thirst after righteousness: for they shall be filled" (Matthew 5:6). Sid and Larry have hungry hearts for everything that is good and beneficial. They are passionate in their love for the Lord Jesus and desire to know Him more. Their hunger for righteousness spills over into other areas as well, such as their vocations. If a new skill needs to be learned for their work, they don't have to be told—chances are they are already studying it. They will never be left behind in their jobs since they are always out in front of everyone else.

What is your attitude about learning? Are you only willing to learn what interests you, or do you have a general hunger to learn? What gets you excited? Is it memorizing details on the sports page or new turkey calling techniques? What about digging into God's Word? Whatever attitude you have, whether you realize it or not, is leaving an impression on your children.

A joy and interest in learning is a great heritage I received from my parents. They are like children in a candy shop when it comes to learning something that is new and beneficial. My mom is skilled at plumbing, wiring, home repair, and fine-art painting. My dad can do just about anything as well, and despite being in his seventies, he keeps right on learning. He even took a job as a computer salesman because he wanted to learn about computers. How many people that age want to have anything to do with computers?

We should be grateful we even have the privilege to learn. "For the LORD giveth wisdom: out of his mouth *cometh* knowledge and understanding" (Proverbs 2:6). If we are hungry to learn and pass that example to our children, it will bless them for the rest of their lives.

## Godly Character

We have seen how character has a tremendous influence on a man's ability to adequately provide for his family. A man's character will greatly affect his income and his expenses. Character is the essence of a man.

Troy, Sid, Scott, Larry, and Dave are excellent examples of men with character. Their incomes vary greatly and so do their needs. Yet none of them suffer want because God provides for all of their needs. These men's ages vary greatly, and they are not all at the same place in their character development. However, they are growing in character as we all should.

Not only must we set an example of godly character for our children, we must endeavor to make strong, positive character a way of life for them. There are many character-related resources available that may be helpful. However, I encourage you not to overlook the best curriculum of all—the Bible. As you are leading your family altar time, look for examples and verses that highlight character. Emphasize one character trait for a week or longer. Whatever you choose to do, be faithful at it. Don't give up simply because the results don't appear immediately.

It is all too easy to relegate certain training aspects to others and consider it their responsibility. Whether it is a school, a church, a tutor, or your spouse, you must not lose sight of the fact that the father is ultimately responsible before God for his children. "For the husband is the head of the wife, even as Christ is the head of the church: and he is the saviour of the body" (Ephesians 5:23). The minute details of how you train your children in character are not so important as the fact that you are putting forth effort. Your persistence in character training, demonstration of that character in your life, and prayer will ground your children's character.

Without this, our children will end up poor witnesses for Christ. Dan considers himself a good witness for Christ because he has a real zeal to share Christ with others. Unfortunately, within his company, he is seen as lazy, undependable, and a waste of company funds. Through the years I have known quite a few men like Dan. Their poor character is a blotch on the name of Christ. Their families will suffer because of their poor income and wasteful spending. May we be committed to raising real men of God.

## View of Work

Preparing a son to provide for his family begins with instilling in him a Biblical view of work. God created the garden to be perfect; therefore, we can assume it reflected His best for man. Let's look closer and see what we can learn from God's plan for man in the garden. "And the LORD God took the man, and put him into the Garden of Eden to dress it and to keep it" (Genesis 2:15). The Hebrew word for "dress" means to work and serve. We are here to work and serve in accordance with God's purpose for man.

Work is not punishment. It is a gift. "Every man also to whom God hath given riches and wealth, and hath given him power to eat thereof, and to take his portion, and to rejoice in his labour; this *is* the gift of God" (Ecclesiastes 5:19). Talk to a man who has been out of work for a while and has just recently found a job. Unless he is a sluggard, he will say God has blessed him with work again.

I expect the majority of Christian men view work as the vehicle that God uses to provide for his family. If that is so, why have

I heard so many of them complain about going to work? How could we ever grumble against God's provision for the needs of our family? "But if any provide not for his own, and specially for those of his own house, he hath denied the faith, and is worse than an infidel" (1 Timothy 5:8).

Serving is also clearly another of God's purposes for man. Whether we are serving an employer, our family, or others, we are to put forth effort and enjoy doing so. If we rejoice in serving and teach our children the same, we have given them a marvelous heritage. The man who finds his joy in serving has the potential for a lifetime of joy. But the man whose joy is in entertainment finds his joy is dependent entirely on the size of his income.

As our society continues its downward character slide, there are fewer men who appreciate work and are willing to work. Those who do not want to work still expect an ever-increasing wage for inferior effort. Sadly, hard workers are a species in danger of extinction!

Think about how important it is for parents to set a godly work example for coworkers and family members. Try being a cheerful, hard worker. Others will notice, including your sons!

How does a child learn to enjoy working? By our example and by working himself. We do our children no favor by not teaching them to enjoy work. Simple.

## How Sure Is Your Foundation?

Incorporating the essence of this chapter first into a parent's life and then the son's life is critical to that son having a sure foundation on which to build his life. Starting with the assurance of salvation, your foundation will be firm. Building the disciplines of daily time with the Lord in Bible reading and prayer develops your dependence on the Lord Jesus and your knowledge of His Word and His ways.

A father's contentment or discontentment with his income is discernible by a son and will greatly shape that son's ability to be content with his wages. Understanding we are stewards accountable to the Master impacts our ability to make choices concerning our possessions and our care for them. When a father desires to be pleasing to the Lord, he knows he is heading his son in the right direction as well.

Dad's hunger to learn will influence the ever-watchful heart of an admiring son. The parent's character is reflected in his children. Finally, as a son observes his father live a Scripturally justified personal view of work, that son will find himself automatically pulled to the same view of work. How sure is your foundation?

## Questions

1. Are you assured of your salvation?

2. Do you have a daily time of personal Bible reading and prayer? If not, when, where, and how could you begin?

3. Are you studying the Bible? If not, what needs to happen so that you will?

4. Are you teaching the Bible to your family? If not, what needs to happen so that you will?

5. Are you memorizing Scripture? If not, what needs to happen so that you will?

6. Evaluate your character qualities, both positive and negative. How do they affect your work? How do you see them reflected in your sons?

7. What is your view of work? How have you communicated it to your sons, verbally and nonverbally?

8. Think about God's purposes for work. Can you think of more? How does this understanding affect you ability to provide for your family? How will it affect your son's ability to provide for his family?

---

By the way, I can find no example of anyone in the
Bible who abided by a forty-hour week. Not Jesus,
not Paul, not any of the Apostles, not any of the
Prophets, and not one single person in the Hebrews
11 "Faith Hall of Fame" to whom we are told to look
as our examples. Not one! And I also am not aware
that there is any age distinction recognized on this
issue anywhere in the Bible (that adults should learn
to love labor but children shouldn't).
*David Barton*

Man is born to work, and he must work
while it is day. "Have I not," said a great
worker, "an eternity to rest in?"
*Tynman*

---

# Appetites

---

*For, brethren, ye have been called unto*
*liberty; only use not liberty for an occasion*
*to the flesh, but by love serve one another.*
*Galatians 5:13*

---

Appetites! Perhaps this is the most difficult chapter in the entire book. It may pierce the heart of many a parent as it pierces my own heart. Appetites strike at my areas of hypocrisy and weakness. Appetites can negatively impact a man's ability to provide for his family, not to mention causing his wife heartache and himself difficulty. As parents we innately have the God-given role of influencing our children's appetites. This influence will be in the direction of developing either positive appetites or negative ones. Since these appetites directly impact a son's ability to provide for his family, let's spend this chapter digging into this "forbidden" and touchy subject. My prayer is that you will be open to consider and evaluate the thoughts and concerns brought up in this chapter.

## What Could Be Wrong with That?

When Randy was five, his mother taught him to play a little card game. It was called "Penny Pat," having the objective of winning the other person's pennies. What started out as an innocent gesture of love by a mother desiring to spend time with her son soon led her son to a passion for gambling. Within years he was addicted. School held little interest. A seemingly innocuous game led to an enslaving passion. How would this have affected Randy's ability to care for his family had Randy, as an adult, not come to know Jesus Christ as his Savior and been freed from the chains of gambling?

Teri and I have chosen never to try downhill skiing. Is skiing sinful? No, of course not! Perhaps we thought it would not be fun? No. We knew it would be an exciting way to enjoy the winter outdoors. However, friends have told us how expensive a hobby skiing is, and we saw no reason to create an appetite in ourselves for it.

In Scripture we see that an appetite will drive a man. "He that laboureth laboureth for himself; for his mouth craveth it of him" (Proverbs 16:26). God gave us appetites for a reason: they are great motivators! Hunger motivates us to work. Unfortunately, there is a negative side to appetites. Dr. S.M. Davis in his video, "How to Train Children to Refuse Evil and Choose Good" (www.drsmdavis.com), phrases it this way, "Starve the bad appetites, and feed the good ones." Appetites, when fed, become passions!

Our appetites are powerful forces within us, and they have to be managed, even if the appetite is for something not considered blatant sin. We must resist everything that isn't God's best for us and for our children.

Appetites grow out of our desires. We must understand that our hearts' desires cannot be trusted unless they fully line up with Scripture. "The heart *is* deceitful above all *things*, and desperately wicked: who can know it?" (Jeremiah 17:9). That is why we take captive every thought to make it obedient to Christ (2 Corinthians 10:5).

Flying small private planes was a passion for me. I acquired my appetite for flying from my father. I fed it, and it became a passion. Twenty years ago my Lord Jesus told me no more flying. God spoke to my heart about discontinuing since I had to take a significant amount of our limited family income to fly each month. There is nothing sinful about flying; it just wasn't God's best for me.

## The Financial Impact

My flying took money that was needed to support my family. That is not uncommon. The husband takes money God has given for the family's needs and spends it on his own desires.

Even though a wife agrees to the expenditures doesn't mean she believes it is God's best use for the money. When I was spending the family's money on flying, it was okay with Teri. She said, "Yes," because she loved me and wanted me to be happy.

Sometimes men may even whine and subtly pout when they don't get their way. Eventually the wife will say, "Go ahead." In a flash we have spent the money with our wives' "full" blessing. We must remember, though: even if we can finagle our wives into agreeing doesn't mean it is the Lord's will.

Are we committed to wanting God's best for our families and ourselves? Have we considered the financial consequences our appetites may bring on our families? Not only can our appetites be harmful for us, but they can also fuel negative appetites in our children. What will it be? Will we choose to feed the good appetites and starve the bad ones?

## Don't Stir Bad Appetites

Jesus said, "No servant can serve two masters: for either he will hate the one, and love the other; or else he will hold to the one, and despise the other. Ye cannot serve God and mammon" (Luke 16:13). "For ye are bought with a price: therefore glorify

God in your body, and in your spirit, which are God's" (1 Corinthians 6:20). The simple fact is, Christians are bought and paid for. We are the Lord's servants and must restrict our appetites and activities to those things He chooses for our lives. Then we can know our lives will bring Him glory.

We should be careful not to stir up appetites that will war against God's direction for our lives and our children's. "Dearly beloved, I beseech *you* as strangers and pilgrims, abstain from fleshly lusts, which war against the soul" (1 Peter 2:11). So much grief can be avoided if we will be cautious.

My father allowed certain appetites to be stirred up in my life that have caused me no little grief. Unfortunately, my father is not alone, as I have observed other fathers doing the same with their sons. This is such a serious thing that we fathers need to take the following Scripture as a grave warning: "But whoso shall offend one of these little ones which believe in me, it were better for him that a millstone were hanged about his neck, and *that* he were drowned in the depth of the sea" (Matthew 18:6).

Realizing the seriousness of my influence on my children, I try carefully to guard the appetites that are stirred within them. We must understand that our children's lives will not be ruined if they miss out on some fun experiences. For example, there have been opportunities for my children to go for a private plane ride or a motorcycle ride. I have not pursued any of those offers. Would they have had fun? Absolutely! However, I know that they could have come away "hooked" with an appetite for something that God might not have directed to be a part of their lives. I would love to see God lead one of my children to be a missionary pilot, but I won't take the chance of stirring up a "flying" appetite unless God very clearly directs.

## Can't We Have Any "Fun"?

First seeking God's direction seems to be the missing ingredient in most men's decisions about how they will spend their time. Obviously, I can't see whether a man is earnestly praying or not, but I can observe whether his choices line up with Scripture. Before we do anything, particularly recreation or entertainment related, we should seek our Father's direction. "Father, please tell me how You would have me to spend this time. I'm your servant, and I will do whatever You ask me. Father, I want your best for my life."

I can imagine the Lord giving His blessing on a father and his son being away for some special time of fellowship. Our world is beautiful and nature cries out in praise of the Lord. Unfortunately, I mostly see dads spending hours alone pursuing their hobbies. They are missing out on valuable family time and ignoring responsibilities while wasting money. The son learns from this that life is lived for his hobbies, separation from the family for the pursuit of fun is okay, and "religious" activities can be reserved for Sundays and heaven.

*"I am struggling with the submission issue because my husband has been gone since ten this morning and is likely not to get home until eight or so tonight. This is his weekly routine, to spend the majority of his Saturdays on his hobby. His work schedule does not allow much time for him to be home during the week as he is usually gone for twelve to thirteen hours each day. He does spend Sundays with us, going to church for both morning and evening services, and also on Wednesday night. I know I should not complain, and that I am to be his helpmeet, not vice versa, but I just get so frustrated. I feel that our children need their dad around more. Sometimes he will take our sons*

*with him, but we both agree that it would be easy for*
*one of the boys to get hurt, so this is not something*
*he does often. I just wish he would DESIRE to*
*spend his free time at home with us. I have been*
*praying that he would have this desire, and I have*
*seen some improvement, but I'm still struggling."*
*A Discouraged Mom*

What if someone says, "Just wait a minute! Are you telling me I can't have a good time and enjoy life?" My answer to that would be, "Friend, I guess it depends what it takes for you to have a good time and enjoy life." That is the essence of this chapter. What are your passions and appetites? Are they of the Lord or of the flesh? If they are of the flesh, God will neither sanction them nor bless them. "Thus saith the LORD, What iniquity have your fathers found in me, that they are gone far from me, and have walked after vanity, and are become vain?" (Jeremiah 2:5).

Someone may thoroughly enjoy imitation crabmeat and develop quite an appetite for it until they finally taste the "real thing." There is no greater joy or fulfillment than to see others walking in the truth and to have a part in it. John said, "I have no greater joy than to hear that my children walk in truth" (3 John 1:4). I challenge you to consider obedience to Christ, working, and serving others to be the best, most enjoyable life there is. This is the kind of life you want for your sons and their families.

Let us look at another verse. "For, brethren, ye have been called unto liberty; only *use* not liberty for an occasion to the flesh, but by love serve one another" (Galatians 5:13). We are not to use our freedom in Christ for our own pleasure. Christians are bought with a price. That means they are owned—lock, stock, and barrel. We are only to do what the Father tells us to do. Jesus set the example by only doing what the Father told Him. "Then answered Jesus and said unto them, Verily, verily, I say unto you, The Son can do nothing of himself, but what he seeth the Father do: for what things soever he doeth, these also doeth the Son likewise" (John 5:19).

The question is, "Did the Father tell us to do it?" Jesus said, "And he that sent me is with me: the Father hath not left me alone; for I do always those things that please him" (John 8:29). If we are doing what He tells us, our activities will always be pleasing to Him. "And they that are Christ's have crucified the flesh with the affections and lusts" (Galatians 5:24).

What if someone is tempted to say, "My entertainment is my rest"? "Six days thou shalt do thy work, and on the seventh day thou shalt rest: that thine ox and thine ass may rest, and the son of thy handmaid, and the stranger, may be refreshed" (Exodus 23:12). The Hebrew word for rest means to cease, desist, and rest. Consider whether or not entertainment is truly restful. How often have you spoken to a man on Monday morning only to have him say how tired he was after a weekend of recreation?

Can you see why this chapter is so important? Appetites expose a father's real interests, and his real interests will be impressed on the heart of his son. So in the privacy of our prayer time, may we all evaluate which activities we participate in that are glorifying to the Lord and which ones are not His best and should be done away with.

## Entertainment and Recreation

Our society is addicted to entertainment. We want to sit back and be thrilled. We like our time to pass quickly while our mental fancies are tickled. We have grown up this way. Our parents enjoyed their entertainment, and they have wanted to share it with us as well. What eternal value is gained through entertainment?

Yet billions of dollars are spent on it each year. What if we were to take all the time and money Christians spend on entertainment and channel it toward winning the lost? Now that is exciting!

To help translate this chapter from the realm of philosophy to reality, let's look at some specific appetites we struggle with and will pass on to our children if we do not choose to starve these appetites. Consider with me the impact entertainment appetites will have on a son and his provision, both materially and spiritually, for his family. There is a hobby or club for every interest imaginable. Obviously, we can't cover each of them. I believe, though, as we step down through several of the most common of men's recreations, you will see the patterns emerge.

## Movies

Parents will spend money they don't have to go to movies they should not see, setting a horrible example for their children to follow.

Are we so anxious to be entertained that we will allow our minds to be filled with wrong thoughts and words? "According as he hath chosen us in him before the foundation of the world, that we should be holy and without blame before him in love" (Ephesians 1:4). From what I'm told, movies these days are full of violence, immorality, and profanity. How can a professing Christian allow his mind to be filled with these things? Paul says, "Finally, brethren, whatsoever things *are* true, whatsoever things *are* honest, whatsoever things *are* just, whatsoever things *are* pure, whatsoever things *are* lovely, whatsoever things *are* of good report; if *there be* any virtue, and if *there be* any praise, think on these things" (Philippians 4:8). Think on these things my friends. Not the things the world fills our minds with, but the things in this verse.

Create a passion for entertainment in your child and it will be a lead weight, strapped to his back, keeping him from God's best. Give yourself and your children a life-long gift of extra money by starving the appetite to see movies.

## Television

I don't know which consequence of TV watching is worse, wasting time while feeding the appetite for being entertained, or ingesting the moral sludge that is presented. I believe it also neuters a man's drive to work and serve the Lord. If that weren't true, men accustomed to that diet would not have earned the reputation of being called "couch potatoes." Men of God who are good workers are not "couch potatoes." Parents must ask themselves what type of children they want to raise. "And the cares of this world, and the deceitfulness of riches, and the lusts of other things entering in, choke the word, and it becometh unfruitful" (Mark 4:19).

Let's look at one seemingly harmless aspect of TV—watching game shows. Could it be that the game-show seeds planted through the years are now sprouting into the gambling and lottery craze that has swept our country? The thrill of seeing people "come on down" and win truckloads of wonderful items without having to work leaves a powerful impression. Might a son's desire to work for his needs be replaced by the fantasy of winning the jackpot?

These are all things that need to be considered if we desire to raise men and women of God. We should be aware of how these appetites can decrease our children's earning potential and hamper their work ethic if they have been raised on a diet of being entertained by the TV. It takes a huge paradigm shift to go from wanting to spend time in a stimulating, but mindless, activity to valuing every minute of time and wanting to use it the way the Lord Jesus directs.

May we be true servants of God and not watch a minute of TV more than our Lord commands us to. "Say not ye, There are yet four months, and *then* cometh harvest? behold, I say unto you, Lift up your eyes, and look on the fields; for they are white already to harvest" (John 4:35). Please receive this caution from someone who cares about you and your children's souls. All Christians are accountable to their Lord for how they spend their time. He is the One we must answer to.

## Spectator Sports

Spectator sports seem to be the number one passion of the American male, in and out of the church. Is there anything truly beneficial about spectator sports? It is extremely hard to come up with any benefit gained from watching sports. At best sports are an absolute waste of the precious time we have on earth; at worst, idolatry.

Spectator sports cheapen our time to a worthless commodity. If watching sports is the best use of a man's time, he might as well go on home to be with the Lord. "For, brethren, ye have been called unto liberty; only *use* not liberty for an occasion to the flesh, but by love serve one another" (Galatians 5:13).

By watching and attending spectator sports, consider the appetite you are giving your son to want to be a sports star. He will spend his time dreaming toward and perhaps even preparing to be a professional athlete. His hours could instead be used for learning productive life skills and in Christian service.

If you shelter your sons from alcohol at home, what happens at sporting events? Your child will watch those around him enjoying their beer with great gusto. Might he possibly develop a secret appetite for what is "forbidden" as he quietly observes his fellow sport fans? Consider what such an appetite will cost him financially should he indulge it once he is no longer under your authority. Would a Christian father really want to expose his son to the possibility of developing this appetite?

May we not just go with the flow of our society or church. May we be men of God raising godly seed for our Lord's honor and glory.

## Team Sports

It all starts when they are young and cute. We want the best for them and don't want them to miss out on any wonderful experience. Have Christians really evaluated what they will reap from the years of sowing a child's love of sports? Has the Lord been sought as to whether team sports are truly His direction? Aren't we creating an appetite for spectator sports and all the negative consequences associated with them?

Team sports are generally accepted as a good, proper, and beneficial activity for youth. What about Christian youth? A child only has a limited amount of free time in a week. Have the parents evaluated what the best use of that time is? Consider Proverbs 22:6, "Train up a child in the way he should go: and when he is old, he will not depart from it." Could we not rephrase it, "Give your child a love for team sports, and when he is old he will be a couch potato in love with spectator sports"?

After a workshop one evening, a man discussed with me his son's involvement in team sports. He wanted his son to learn to work hard and with others on a team. I asked him whether he could think of no better way to accomplish these goals.

I have not observed team sports building the proper spirit of teamwork. Rather they foster a spirit of pride. If you want to develop teamwork, have your son work with his siblings on some projects. If he can work with them, he can get along with anyone. If you want him to learn to work hard, take him with you when you help a widow with a home repair. (There will be much more on this in a later section so I won't go further now.)

Nathan and Christopher were great Little League baseball players. They loved baseball, and we loved to watch them play. Going to the games was fun and a real family affair. Practices would begin late February, and games would continue into June. Then if you were "fortunate," your son would be chosen for the All-Star team and participate in another couple of months of practices and games. The end result was an incredible amount of time invested for the whole family.

What did allowing our sons to play baseball cost us? We no longer could set our own schedule. We were at the mercy of the coach to decide where we had to be and when. We no longer controlled whom our sons associated with. They were part of "the team" and were to bond with each other. The greatest price we paid was our evening family altar time.

Family Bible study is very important to me for the development of my family. I value it next in importance to my own Bible reading and prayer time. I now was forced to sacrifice our family altar time to the god of sports. I was choosing to give up my opportunity to teach my children God's Word—the one thing that would have the greatest impact on my sons' ability to lead and provide for their families. Finally, this realization hit home!

Teri and I knew it would be the last baseball season for our sons. After the final game of the season, I took Nathan and Christopher out for a soda. With tears running down my cheeks,

I explained why we were ending team sports for our family. I shared with each of them how much team sports was costing our family and that we could bear it no longer. To my joy, they both accepted my direction. I firmly believe that as a result of this decision, we have seen God pour out unimaginable blessings into our sons' lives.

What about you? Will you consider the consequences of having your children involved in team sports? Are you going to be the one responsible for cultivating an appetite for spectator sports in them? Do you realize the future impact that it can have on your son's ability to be a man of God and provide for his future wife and children?

## Hunting and Fishing

What could be wrong with hunting, fishing, and other similar activities? There are definitely no beer commercials to see while you are out enjoying God's beautiful creation.

Kevin spent all of his extra money and free time hunting, fishing, or working with his gear. It was his passion. His wife didn't go with him because she had her own interests. Kevin is a good example of an appetite turned passion. Could that happen to anyone? Yes, but only God knows who. There is nothing inherently wrong with these types of outdoor sports—unless they take a dad away from his family. If they do, I think a man would have a hard time justifying such activities Scripturally. It might be a good way for a father to be away from the distractions of the city with a child once in a great while. However, like anything, seeking the Lord's direction and self-control are necessary.

## Recreational Vehicles

Dollars, dollars, and more dollars. If boats can be viewed as a hole in the water that you pour money into, then an airplane is like trying to wallpaper the sky with dollar bills. The older a man gets, the more expensive his toys.

If an appetite for recreational or sport vehicles is cultivated, a man will never earn enough money. His joy will always be limited by the size of his income and his relationship with the bank's loan officer. What is the cure? Treat motorcycles, jet skis, ski boats, sailboats, airplanes, and campers as though you were handling nitroglycerin.

Since Dad is often the one in charge of the finances, if he struggles with an appetite for any of these vehicles, he will be sorely tempted to spend family money on his passion. He will have to fight the desire to spend God's resources on the biggest, best, and newest toy.

Recreational vehicles are so addictive. Think about how much time and money can be spent on them. Has the Lord said, "Yes, you are to buy one"? Or has He said, "Yes, because of the hardness of your heart, go ahead." "And Jesus answered and said unto them, For the hardness of your heart he wrote you this precept" (Mark 10:5).

I encourage you to consider the consequences of buying recreational vehicles. If Saturdays are free, is there truly no better use of time than one of these? What sorts of passions are being created in the children and what impact will it have on your son's ability to provide for a family?

## Eating

Ouch. This one really hits close to home. My appetite for food was cultivated when my parents were divorcing, and I turned to food for comfort. As an adult, I was able to mask my appetite by exercising. Unfortunately, with age, as my metabolism has slowed and my knees no longer allow me to run, the calories accumulate around my waist. This is simply an outward evidence of an inward appetite.

My excessive appetite has reproduced itself in several of my children, and all of them will likely struggle with it. The appetites of the parents will affect their children.

Think about all the ways an excessive appetite for eating will negatively affect your children as they grow. It will cause them to want to spend money on worthless treats that will harm their teeth. It will result in poorer health and, over the years, will increase medical spending. Spending will also rise because of eating out more often. Then there is the need to keep "growing" one's wardrobe. There are more consequences, but even these few examples make it clear that an excessive appetite for food will affect a father's ability to provide for his family.

## Vice

Sin is sin, and we are to "put ye on the LORD Jesus Christ, and make not provision for the flesh, to *fulfil* the lusts *thereof*" (Romans 13:14). We are to be so identified with Christ that we have put on His interests and way of life. The sin that entangles the world is not to part of a Christian's life.

"But as he which hath called you is holy, so be ye holy in all manner of conversation; Because it is written, Be ye holy; for I am holy" (1 Peter 1:15-16). The Lord spoke very plainly through

Peter regarding how we are to live. We are to have holy, pure lives before a righteous and holy God. Think how this clearly takes care of many sinful practices that ensnare the soul and bring ruin to families. I am often saddened when I see people in convenience stores buying alcohol and cigarettes, while it is apparent they have little money. Perhaps they are spending money that was to go for their children's food or clothing. Then with the change they are given, they often give it back to buy a lottery ticket or two hoping to strike it rich.

One time, while I was getting gas, the clerk and the customer in front of me were discussing which local casino was their favorite. I couldn't believe it. Here was the gas station clerk, who would have been fortunate to be making eight dollars an hour, wasting her money gambling. My heart was so heavy I could have wept.

We must be ever so careful to protect our children from appetites for vice. There is a local convenience store where I bought gas once. Right by the checkout counter, about belt high, they have a rack of magazines. These magazines had the most lewd, hideous covers on them. I'm sure the cover was within the letter of the law, but here they had pornography right at a child's eye level. What are most children going to do while their parent pays the cashier? I have never gone back in that store and have instructed my family they are not to enter it either.

Later I was speaking to someone who knew the owner of that store. The owner once told him that he was paid handsomely by the magazine distributor to place those magazines just where I had seen them. They were there deliberately to entice children. "But whoso shall offend one of these little ones which believe in me, it were better for him that a millstone were hanged about his neck, and *that* he were drowned in the depth of the sea" (Matthew 18:6).

I know someone who was introduced to pornography by his own father. The father had the magazines in his home, and the boy found them. How horrible for a father to cause the entrapment of his son. I know another young man whose baseball coach introduced him to pornography. The team went to another city to play a championship game and stayed overnight in a hotel. The coach "treated" the team to a stack of magazines for their entertainment. God will judge those men, "and be sure your sin will find you out" (Numbers 32:23).

As parents we must be careful that neither we nor others are the cause of an ungodly appetite snagging our children. I have read letters from moms who are brokenhearted over the videos their husbands were bringing into the home. Fathers must realize that their sin will be visited on their children. God does not punish the children for their father's sin, but the children will likely adopt it from their dads.

Do we want to raise sons that will be mighty men of God and able to provide well for their families? Then we also must be men of God and extremely vigilant in protecting those whom God has entrusted to us.

## A Few of the Good Appetites

After Sid became a Christian, he was encouraged to go soul winning with a friend. He found it a joy that soon became part of his life. Through the years he continued to share Christ at every God-given opportunity, and it became a passion for him. At work Sid was a diligent worker and did not take company time to share his faith. However, he would gladly use his break time to share Jesus Christ when a door was opened. Most other Christians at work considered Sid radical, because he was fearless. I remember the time he gave an impeccable presentation to a customer, all the while wearing his favorite "Jesus" tie. Sid had a passion for sharing Christ.

My youngest sons, Joseph, John, and Jesse, have been accompanying Nathan, Christopher, and I to the City Union Mission the second Saturday of each month. Nathan is the City Union Mission point-of-contact and coordinator for our church's ministry there. For our City Union Mission service, Christopher plays the piano. Nathan, a few other men from church, and I take turns leading the singing and preaching. It is wonderful!

One Saturday afternoon during the preaching, Joseph, who was ten years old, leaned over to me and said, "Dad, I'm having the best time of my life." John, who is two years younger than Joseph, says the second Saturday is his most favorite day of the whole month. Do you know what I want to create in my sons? I want them to have a passion for sharing Christ and spending time together in beneficial activities.

In Chapter Six we looked at foundational building blocks necessary in our lives, and our children's, if they are to be successful providers for their family. Good appetites corresponding to some of the foundational blocks would be:

- Salvation, desire to share Christ
- Personal quiet time, desire for a closer walk with the Lord
- Knowledge of the Bible, desire for His Word
- Stewardship, desire to give to the needs of others
- Pleasing the Lord, desire to please Him
- Hungry soul, desire to know more of what is good and pleasing
- Godly character, desire to be a man of God

This book is filled with examples of good appetites. They require cultivating in order to make them into passions. These good appetites will make you and your children stronger and more secure as men of God. They will increase both their ability and your ability to provide for a family.

## Men of God, Not Men of the World

Christians are not on earth to have a good time fulfilling the lust of the flesh. Let us not be disheartened, though—God does not intend our lives to be drudgery. There is great joy in serving the King! "And the seventy returned again with joy, saying, LORD, even the devils are subject unto us through thy name" (Luke 10:17). "And he that reapeth receiveth wages, and gathereth fruit unto life eternal: that both he that soweth and he that reapeth may rejoice together" (John 4:36).

## Questions

1. List your good appetites. How are you developing these same appetites in your sons?

2. List your bad appetites.

3. How could you begin to starve your bad appetites?

4. How can you make Sunday a true day of rest?

5. Formulate a plan for exchanging bad appetites you have let develop in your sons for good appetites.

6. List your normal daily and weekly activities. How are they building good or bad appetites in your son's life?

---

But even if we should accept that work is
for the mature and not for children, is one
ever too young to begin training in good
virtues and character traits—traits like
industry, hard work, diligent labor, etc.
Should we wait to train our children in
truthfulness and honesty until they
are older? Or in sexual purity? Or in
godliness and holiness? Or in obedience?
Or in respect of parents? Clearly not. So
why make an exception for the very
necessary character trait of the love of labor?
David Barton

---

# Ages Three to Six

---

*. . . to rejoice in his labour; this is the gift of God.*
*Ecclesiastes 5:19*

---

As young as ages three to six, and perhaps even a bit earlier, you will begin the process of training your sons to provide for a single-income family. The training from these early years will be built upon throughout their childhood and relied upon throughout adulthood.

One of the most important training aspects, even at this age, is that time is valuable and not to be wasted. We teach this by occupying our children productively as opposed to constantly entertaining them. We can allow our young children to be "Daddy's little helpers" and also to have their own chores, while limiting activities that will lean toward an entertainment mentality. These will be the beginning steps toward helping a child learn to value time and not waste it.

## Spiritually

Most of my children have come to know Jesus as their Lord and Savior around the ages of five and six. Be careful not to push a child or coerce him toward salvation in any way. For your child to recite a salvation prayer without a change of heart does no one any good.

Six-year-old Jesse was our most recent child to be saved. He had been mentioning for several months that the Lord was talking to him about salvation. Each time he came to me, I told him that was great, and we could talk about it when he was ready. I wanted to make sure this wasn't "false labor." I waited until he couldn't be put off any longer. Finally, he came to me and said, "Dad, I really want to talk to you about being saved. Can we talk about it now?" I said we would discuss it after supper.

We went down into my office and closed the door. I asked Jesse a number of questions to determine if he really understood what the Lord had done for him. Did he understand sin and the consequences of it? Did he understand the Cure for sin? Was he able to earn salvation in any way? After I was satisfied he had a good comprehension of salvation, I asked him to go to his room and pray about whether he really wanted to become a Christian. He came back eight minutes later and said he was sure.

I then asked if he liked people telling him what to do. He said, "No." I explained that salvation meant Jesus becoming his boss. I asked Jesse to go pray again about whether he really was willing to make Jesus his boss. He went away and came back four minutes later. "Yes!" he wanted Jesus to be his boss. I asked whether he would like to have Mom with us when he prayed, and he thought that would be a good idea. We went upstairs to the living room and knelt at the sofa. I prayed for him, and then led him in prayer. At that moment, Jesse Maxwell became a child of God.

Dear friend, this is where it all begins. Do you want your son to be able to provide for his family? Then he must be a son of "The Provider." When your son is living in obedience to his Lord, he is in good hands. Just as the natural birth of our sons had no predetermined, exact time, Scripture tells us of no specific age when a child can become a Christian. We watch for the signs, remain constant in prayer, and lay the groundwork. Then what joy is ours as parents when God speaks to their hearts and calls them to be His own!

## Serving

What could be a better use of time than to bring a young son along as you help someone? My children are happy to go wherever Daddy goes. It doesn't get any better than when they can be with Dad and learn how fun it is to help someone.

Raising young children is a lot of work, and there might not be that much extra time for outside serving. However, if there is no entertainment, it is likely there will be some time available for serving others.

Teri's parents live next door to us, and the children have opportunities to help them. I love it when a young one spies Granddad outside trimming bushes and wants to go over to help. At this age they aren't a lot of help, but it builds in them the desire to serve.

## Daddy's Little Helper

I have very fond memories of my boys and me building bedrooms in our basement. Nathan and Christopher were in their teens, but Joseph and John were five and three respectively. The older boys were great assets to me as they learned important skills, while Joseph and John had the time of their lives not even realizing they were "in training."

The little guys, trying to imitate us older workers, would put on whatever appropriate apparatus they could find. They would adorn themselves with hearing protectors, safety glasses, dust masks, suspenders, and work belts. Then they would grab the nearest hammer, even if it was the one I had momentarily put down. Joseph was able to actually drive nails but I think John just pounded. I had to keep an eye on John as he didn't care what he pounded; he just wanted to hammer something. If anyone ever pulls the sheetrock off our basement walls, they will find hundreds of nails in the footers. They might not understand how important those nails were. They were a necessary part of a young boy learning to hammer a nail in straight, learning that work can give you a feeling of accomplishment, and learning that work is fun when you are with your daddy. Those two little boys loved "help'un" Dad and still do!

That is why these early ages are so important. You have the opportunity to shape your son's attitude regarding work. Whatever you are doing, as long as it is not dangerous, you should have your son with you. Not only are you building a heart bond with that son, but you are also helping him associate positive memories with work.

As your children work with you, keep in mind how important it is to make it a good experience, and be careful not to frustrate them. "And, ye fathers, provoke not your children to wrath: but bring them up in the nurture and admonition of the LORD" (Ephesians 6:4). Be gentle, loving, and kind without criticism because your purpose is for them to want to help Daddy again.

It is also important that they are allowed to actually "help." Have you ever volunteered at a poorly organized church-work project when there were no meaningful work assignments being given? It is boring to sit around and watch someone else do all the work. In the same way, if your children aren't allowed to "work," they are not going to want to "work" with you again.

This morning while our family was over working at Nathan's house, six-year-old Jesse spent the longest time picking up sticks in the yard and bringing them to me. He was so pleased to be able to help, and he was performing a needed task. One of my jobs was to break the sticks up into small pieces for the trash bag. He loved seeing the pile of sticks continue to grow before me. We had great "fun." Joseph and John, though older now, were also over there gladly working with us.

There is something special about men working and fellowshipping together. My boys have found that hard work becomes pleasurable when you are working alongside another.

## Proper Expectations

I have discovered that I get more than I bargained for when I have young children helping me on projects. If the project has any degree of difficulty, I have the opportunity to work on my character! You see, I become impatient when trying to answer a million questions while concentrating on my work. Little boys ask questions like, "Daddy, why did you break that bolt off?" or, "Why can't we do it this way?" If I don't mentally prepare for the fact that the task will take longer with my sons' participation, I will become frustrated. Then, instead of having a wonderful shared time, we are both unhappy. Therefore, make sure you begin a project with proper expectations.

## Pay Special Attention to Safety

It is crucial that we be extra cautious regarding our children's safety when they are helping us on projects. Consider precautions such as unplugging the power tools after use, keeping anything sharp out of little ones' reach, and leaving no climbing temptations that could result in a fall. I don't let the boys on ladders until they are older, as I haven't found a good way to protect them. You will find the extra time and effort spent assuring your child's safety well worth it.

A family we know shared with us how one of their young sons stuck a drill up his younger brother's nose and pulled the trigger. The mom said she had never seen anything bleed so profusely. Please do not underestimate your child's ability to do something he shouldn't. Exercise much caution.

A good way to double-check yourself is to ask your wife if she sees a danger you might have overlooked. If she has any additional concerns, they should be resolved.

## Simple Chores

I have heard some parents say that they want their children to have fun being children. Therefore, they don't want them to work. My question is, "Just when do they learn to work?" God has called us to work, and we are especially blessed if we can enjoy working. That is why it is good to find ways to teach our children to work. One way we can do this is by assigning them simple chores. From an early age, we begin assigning our children daily chores. Sure, these jobs require time on our part, first training the children in what to do and then daily inspecting, but it is well worth the effort!

When Mary was three, Teri assigned her a few easy chores: setting the table, putting her clothes away, and making her bed. They were simple tasks that Mary could do and then feel a sense of satisfaction in completing them. She was so cute. Here was this little sweetie putting the napkins on the table with a smile on her face as she did her chores just like the older children. She was proud of what she accomplished and was performing a needed family service.

At five we purchased Jesse a little dustpan and brush. He was responsible for keeping the stray dog food swept up three times a day.

On our family's website, www.Titus2.com, we have listed children's ages and chores from many real-life families. You may find it helpful to be able to see what chores various aged children are doing in other homes when evaluating your own children's chore assignments.

I encourage you to begin training your child at an early age to be responsible with assigned tasks. It is good for them to learn to work and be counted on to help the family. That is worthwhile "teamwork"!

## Allowance

Teri and I believe it is good for a child to have an allowance, unless you have other ways he can earn money on a regular basis. The dollar amount of the allowance can be quite low, just enough to help the child purchase gifts throughout the year. In our family, two or more children will usually go together to purchase a gift, which helps their small allowance to last through the year.

The children also receive gift money. In addition, they occasionally have opportunities to earn additional money for discretionary purchases. At this age, Teri and I exercise total control over what the child spends his money on. We have found that giving a child an allowance is a good way to begin introducing him to handling money.

## Television

We know how difficult it can be to manage a home with little ones, and that is one reason why our book *Managers of Their Homes* has been so well received. It is a strong temptation for a mother to let the TV baby-sit the children. Don't think that it would be nice to have the children occupied in front of the TV. Rather, you must remember how harmful it is to create an appetite for entertainment. Children will be far less likely to be creative with their time when they have access to a TV. When they grow up, creative children make valued workers.

Just this week Sarah read to me a mom's message from one of the Titus2 message boards. The family had been off TV for three weeks, and the mom could not believe the positive changes she was seeing in her children. She mentioned how one of her children had a learning disability. To her surprise, that child's behavior was greatly improved.

If you choose to let your child watch videos, then I have a few cautions. Only let him watch them on rare occasions such as a holiday or when he is ill. Get rid of all cartoon or humanistic videos. If a child is going to watch something, let it be either educational or devotional.

Every parent must search his heart and raise this TV issue before the Lord. For hundreds of years families have been raising children without a TV or videos. Will TV's impact to your son's future be worth the trade-off today? This is a question that certainly deserves careful attention.

## Computer

Many Christian families have discovered the computer can take the place of time spent watching TV. Unfortunately, if the computer is not managed correctly, it can introduce as many negatives as a TV.

We have chosen not to purchase computer games because of the negative appetites they develop. Most educational programs are more "game" than educational because they are designed to appeal to the average child. Unfortunately, that means the software was created for a child who has been raised on TV. It requires a lot of "razzle dazzle" to hold their interest. We want our children to think of the computer as a tool not a toy.

When one of our children expresses an interest and is showing some manual dexterity, we will let him begin to type. At six years of age, Jesse was mastering both reading and typing. He spent many hours using the typing program and word processor. Think about it. Here was a six-year-old boy having a great time learning. We have found that it does not require foolish, eye-catching graphics for a child to learn new skills. If you teach your child using all of the stimulating "eye candy," then be prepared to keep it up as he grows older. Why not let him find out how good it is to learn without all of the glitz?

This is a very important concept for you to grasp. The benefits in a child's life will never stop if he is able to learn on his own. Later, when he has graduated from high school, he won't have to be enticed or spoon-fed to learn. It may make the difference between your spending vast amounts of money on instructor-led classes versus your son being able to dig information out of a textbook on his own. This concept is foundational and can pay huge dividends throughout your child's life.

When Mary was four she would spend hours using the "Paint" program that came with the computer. It isn't much different from drawing with "electronic" crayons, but she was teaching herself about the computer by using it. She was at ease with the computer and finding learning to be enjoyable. As long as children don't have access to games, real learning is very attractive to them. It can help build the right kind of appetites for their future.

I had no idea there were so many children's websites on the Internet. On the message board located at our website, www.Titus2.com, a number of moms suggested children's websites. Since it is a moderated board, we had to visit each site before approving the post. My observation was that these were mostly Internet game sites and had no real benefit. I would encourage you to apply the same rule to websites as you do to computer programs—NO GAMES!

A special caution is in order regarding Internet use. It seems that everyone is aware of the morality-destroying websites that are out there. Do not allow your children to surf the Internet. If you must, only allow it when a parent is present, and be very cautious about which sites are visited. Wolves will impersonate a common website address by changing the suffix or a few letters in the name, hoping to snag careless surfers. Once you have checked a site out, add it to your favorites so there is no danger of mistyping the address and landing at an awful place. How much caution and trouble on your part is the purity of your child's mind worth to you?

## Team Sports

It seems like team sports' "opportunities" are now available to children at earlier and earlier ages. Even if a Christian group offers team sports, it is still creating an appetite for sports that will stay with the child. Think about how many wives wish their husbands did not watch team sports. Consider all the wasted hours it consumes in a year. Wouldn't you love to hear your future daughter-in-law call you blessed for not introducing sports into your son's life?

## Training at an Early Age

Is it your goal for your son to be able to adequately provide for his family with one income? If so, you have just read several important ways you can facilitate that. In addition, there are key attitudes you should adopt as you work with him at this early age.

You should be prepared to be diligent. It will require extra effort on your part to fill his time if you do not allow him to seek entertainment. The good news is that your son will become creative, accustomed to learning, and able to occupy himself. Others will be amazed at his maturity, even at a young age.

You must be steadfast. He will see others who are allowed to participate in many things he cannot. How will you respond to his requests? Will you only say "no," or will you be giving of yourself and spend time with him instead? You will find it necessary to protect your son when he is at other children's homes, as he will be drawn to their entertainment. Most are dependent on entertainment, and you can expect that if your son is in their home, he will be offered entertainment as well.

You must be cautious. Picture entertainment and slothfulness as deadly, crippling foes that seek to win your son. The more of your son's heart entertainment wins, the larger the salary he will need to earn to pay for it. Why sow those seeds? What is your commitment level? This really is the bottom line. Are you prepared to include your son with you when you work and serve? Is your heart turned to his? Next to your wife, are your children your best friends? Are you willing to get rid of the TV even though you may consider it a personal sacrifice? Be a man of God who serves the Lord and works hard so that you can be a good example for your son to emulate.

As you continue through this book, please keep in mind that what is written about in one section will carry on to the following age groups. To avoid redundancy, I will not address an area again unless I have new material to present on the topic. However, the building blocks of preparing your son in one age-group, will continue to be applicable for later years as well.

## Questions

1. Are you striving to make Jesus known to your children?

2. Do your children know Jesus personally as their Savior? If not, what are you doing to prepare them for that time?

3. What projects can you think of that your younger sons could work on with you?

4. What simple chores have you given your sons who are in this age group? Are there new ones they are ready for? If so, what are they?

5. What opportunities have you given your sons to serve? Can you think of more?

6. In what other ways can a young boy's learning impact his ability to provide for his future family?

———————————

By withholding work from children when
they are young, I believe that parents may be
acting from several erroneous assumptions:
that children must "enjoy" their childhood
and therefore work is not compatible with
childhood; that work is not or cannot be fun;
and that the Bible does not address this
issue. None of these assumptions is correct,
nor has the fruit of such assumptions proven
beneficial in our society.

*David Barton*

———————————

# Ages Seven to Twelve

---

*. . . for my heart rejoiced in all my labour . . .*
*Ecclesiastes 2:10*

---

Training your son during these years of his life will have a major bearing on his desire to work during his teens. The potentially tumultuous teen stage is weathered upon the foundation you build from ages seven through twelve. Lay the proper foundation, and you will have something to build upon with confidence. Neglect the foundation, and you will spend much time trying to stabilize a "leaning tower."

These are good years to be watching your son and praying. What is his natural bent? What are his God-given talents? What are his weaknesses? What leading is God giving you during your prayer times?

The parents' commitment to preparing their son to provide for his family with a single income becomes increasingly important in this age range. How committed are you to your son's future career success? It will become very obvious during these years. Why? Because as he grows older there will be an increasing amount of pressure as you make difficult decisions that affect his attitude toward work and learning.

## Spiritually

Your son may already be saved by this age. If he isn't, I implore you to make his salvation the cry of your heart. Most of my children have come to know Christ as Lord and Savior before they reach seven years old. Then, after they are saved, they must be fed spiritually. The world will exert a strong pull, and they need to be well grounded in Christ as the attraction begins.

Do you remember the three-legged stool analogy and what each leg stands for? First our example, then what we teach, and finally prayer. Our children are looking at our example of life in Christ and evaluating whether it is something good and desirable. Let them see their Dad excited about God's Word. We must be teaching during family altar time about how Scripture tells us to live and about the foundations we discussed in Chapter Six.

Now is also the time for children to establish the habit of daily Bible reading and prayer. If you have your children's hearts, they will want to have a quiet time like Dad and Mom. They will receive your encouragement to read God's Word and pray. We have found that we can help our children be consistent in their quiet time by making it a part of their morning routine.

## What Is Your Vision?

What purpose for life have you laid before your family as a result of studying God's Word? Do your children see themselves as ambassadors for Christ? Even at this age, when children know they have a "mission," they have purpose in life. "Where *there is* no vision, the people perish: but he that keepeth the law, happy *is* he" (Proverbs 29:18).

Our first priority is training sons and daughters to be men and women of God. As we saw in Malachi 2:15, that is God's purpose for marriage. "And did not he make one? Yet had he the residue of the spirit. And wherefore one? That he might seek a godly seed." Have that purpose before you constantly. Remind your children of it often. Discuss it with your spouse, and cry out to God for His direction for and intercession in your children's lives. Almost every night as I pray with my young sons, I'm asking God to make them men of God. They hear the cry of my heart as I seek God's hand, asking Him to mold them.

In His timing, God will then begin to use your family to serve others. He is glorified when families serve Him. "Let your light so shine before men, that they may see your good works, and glorify your Father which is in heaven" (Matthew 5:16). There is something special about seeing a family serving together harmoniously. It is the "Amen" to the truth of Scripture. The Lord Jesus Christ does make a difference when He is the Lord of a home, and the lost will recognize that. It isn't something to be flaunted, but rather lived. Our world is amazed when it sees mature, responsible children. The purpose is not for people to notice and praise us; instead, it is to bring praise to the King.

If you don't have any serving opportunities, don't worry. Simply pray. God will direct you to them! For example, eight years ago God led our family to conduct semimonthly church services for residents of a local nursing home. During a portion of the service, Christopher plays the piano while we sing hymns. However, I've been grooming twelve-year-old Joseph to take Christopher's place. Joseph has been learning to play the piano for six years. Over the last several months, I have asked Joseph to play a hymn each time we are at the nursing home. There have even been a few weeks when Christopher was not available. Then Joseph accompanied all our singing. He's a bit rough, but so was Christopher when he began playing for us. Start grooming your child to serve.

If your son is taking music lessons, I would encourage you to be sure he is using the talent in a meaningful way.

If you have a heart that desires to serve others, in His time, God will provide the opportunities. Be patient and don't try to rush it. When God has the right ministry for your family, all or most of the family will be able to participate. Your children will be using their talents while learning that there is incredible joy in serving others.

## Instilling the Desire to Do Their Best

I recently needed a crown on one of my teeth. Part of the process involved placing a temporary crown on the tooth while the real crown was being fabricated. Doctor Pete had to hone the temporary crown to just the right height in order to avoid creating a "bite" problem. I sensed he was experiencing some time pressure due to my visit in the middle of a full schedule. However, he resisted the temptation to hurry and was meticulous in getting the temporary crown right. Even though this was not permanent, he kept testing, honing, and retesting to achieve a perfect fit. Doctor Pete is a man who gives his best. The challenge for us is: how do we teach our children to do their best without them feeling like they can't please us?

I'm constantly trying to find the balance that encourages the children to try harder while not discouraging them over what they have done. There have been times I have seen my son's spirit "deflating" when I was encouraging him to redo a project. I know then that I've gone too far. It is time to regroup and start "pumping" him up a bit.

Consider how we are working against "the flesh" in helping our sons learn to give their best. Mankind is lazy and self-centered.

It takes a great deal of effort to train a child to be careful and always do his best. That is a formidable challenge for parents.

I believe two aspects are key to helping your son learn to do his best. First, as I have stressed time and again, we must keep our son's heart. He should look to his parents as the most important people in his life. He needs to trust that they want his best more than anything. He must want to please his parents in everything he does. Friend, you have to keep your child's heart!

Second, we must praise and encourage him on. When Teri and I were first married, my form of exercise was running. I became interested in running a marathon. During preparation for my first marathon, I injured my knee and was forced to stop running for a couple of months while it healed. Unfortunately, when I was able to run again, I did not have sufficient time to be properly conditioned for the race. As youth would have it, I ran that marathon anyway. I don't think I was ever so sick or hurt so badly as during that race! There was one bright spot, though. My sweet wife made every effort to keep ahead of me by driving to points along the race route. When I arrived, there she would be, by the side of the road, cheering me on and encouraging me to keep going. Friend, that is exactly what we must be doing for our sons!

## More Work and Less Play

Every Christian man should expect to spend the majority of his day working and serving. Isn't it reasonable that as our sons approach manhood, they shift toward more work and less play? If so, then why is this the age range when their entertainment level begins increasing? Boys see all the fun things our world offers, and they want to participate like everyone else their age. There will be tremendous peer pressure from relatives, neighbors, and even the church. This is your opportunity to show how committed you are to the goal of preparing your son to be the provider for a single-income family.

It is crucial, though, that you don't take everything your son considers fun away from him without substituting other activities in return. We must give our children the best we have to offer—ourselves. If we have our children's hearts and they have ours, spending time together is as good as it gets!

By spending time with our sons, we avoid some of the negative behavior that most boys this age exhibit. Have you observed how silly preteen boys can be when they get together? The truth of Scripture becomes very obvious. "Foolishness *is* bound in the heart of a child" (Proverbs 22:15). If you want a mature son, have him spend time with you. If you want a foolish son, let him spend quantities of time with boys his own age.

Take your son with you on errands, when you do projects, and when you serve. If you are self-employed, let him come with you whenever possible. I love working from home. When we have completed a large project, we often need to deliver it in Kansas City. I bring one or more of the "little boys" with me, and we become the delivery team, "Rob, Bob, and Bud." Only with the Lord and Dad can something so mundane become such a glorious time for all.

If you have your son's heart, he will prefer to spend time with you over anyone else. Let him see that work is pleasurable; that you enjoy it, and that he can as well. Frankly, there is nothing quite like the fellowship of a man working with his son.

## Significant Chores

Chores are a necessary part of life. They certainly are important for keeping a home in order. Truly, many hands make light work! There is no reason why children in this age range can't be working right alongside Dad and Mom.

One of the many benefits of chores is that our children will appreciate how much work it is to keep house. We do not want to be guilty of raising a son who takes the work his wife does for granted. He should know how to help his wife with household chores in addition to being grateful for all she does.

Children in this age range are capable of accomplishing quite a variety of chores. As I mentioned earlier, check out www.Titus2.com for suggestions on which chores other families are having their children be responsible for doing.

The parents' tenacity is key to children successfully becoming accountable for chores. First, we must not expect them to know how to properly perform a job without training. It may take the child some practice sessions, while Dad or Mom coaches, to be sure he is thoroughly trained. Then it will take our effort to be sure the work is done to the standard. At times it will simply seem easier to do the work yourself, but resist that temptation! Remember, the stakes are far bigger than simply having a task performed correctly. We are training our children to be quality workers—men who can be given a job, who will do their best to complete it on time, and who will function to a higher standard than expected.

Don't think chore training is an easy, overnight process. "And let us not be weary in well doing: for in due season we shall reap, if we faint not" (Galatians 6:9). If training children to be responsible and diligent with their chores were easy, our world would be a different place!

## Real Projects

I am not aware of much that gives a boy a greater sense of accomplishment than letting him do a project by himself! Be alert for tasks that "cry out" for a son's help.

Teri is catching on to this and often asks ten-year-old John to help her. Recently the light bulbs in both hallway fixtures needed to be replaced. This project involved climbing a ladder, and that is something John loves to do. By changing the light bulbs, John did his mother a great service, and she lavished praise on him for helping. He even received a double dose of that praise, because when I came up for dinner, Teri commended John to me for his helpfulness.

Teri has been able to find quite a few other tasks, as well, that the children are able to do for her. Most of them don't take very long, but the children come away feeling good about having done some real work!

When Joseph was seven years old and John was five, they asked if they could landscape the front of the house. The job involved digging up sod in the heat of summer. After some persistence on their part, I agreed to give them the project. I was concerned about the shovels and tools they would be using so I presented them with some rules aimed at protecting them from injury. Every day, out those two little boys would go with their shovels, digging and sweating. I helped them at times, but it was their project. For the final steps, we worked together putting the black weed preventer down and then planting the bushes. I cannot imagine a trophy on a shelf meaning more to me than that landscaping!

Many homeschool families are responsible for organizational newsletters. Why not give your son some responsibility in producing it? Don't begin by trying to decide if your son has the skills for the job. If you approach training your son that way, he will seldom be qualified for anything. In our home the rule is: "If you haven't done something before, or think it is impossible, then we will give you a little more time to do it." Set high goals and learning expectations for your children.

How many of you as adults have been required to do something that you have never done before? I'm confident everyone has had this experience. It's a part of life, isn't it? Therefore, why not get your children accustomed to doing projects that they have never done before? When I ask my child to undertake a new task, I will facilitate him slightly. I want to see him thinking about how he will tackle the job and what he may need to learn before he can begin. He needs to be able to do whatever research is required. There is no reason for a son to be spoon-fed unless you are planning on being by his side when he is providing for his family. If you want a son who is an independent adult, he must learn how to learn on his own and be willing to tackle unknown projects when necessary.

Clearly, I would not tell my eight-year-old to figure out how to design a newsletter. But I might begin by asking him to type in an article for me or look through clip art books to find some appropriate graphics. Over time I would want him to be able to add the graphics to the newsletter and then move on to more difficult newsletter production tasks. Begin where your child is and continue to challenge him. Praise him and let him show his work to others. Ask him to think of ways he might improve on what he has done.

## Tools

If you are able to ensure your children's safety, give them tools. Real tools make great gifts, and if they are of good quality, you are building a tool chest your son will need in the future.

The most memorable wedding present Teri and I received was an electric drill. It wasn't a big deal to her, but I sure liked it! I did not already have many tools of my own, and I used the drill often. I think I would have been better prepared for the responsibilities of maintaining a home and automobile had I received tools as gifts through my childhood and teen years.

Teri and I like to give our sons tools on special, gift-giving occasions. The tools we choose usually have lifetime warranties so we know they are built to last. If the tool ever breaks, it can be exchanged. Screwdrivers, pliers, sockets, and wrenches are all great gifts. How thrilling to a little boy's heart to help Daddy with home repairs using his own tools! As always, it is critical that great caution is exercised to be sure tools are used safely. I have my sons keep their tools put away until Dad is available to work with them.

A while back, our twenty-year-old storm door decided to break. After replacing it, we needed to discard the old one. This was an excellent project for nine-year-old John. He rounded up the tools he needed, and on his own, he determined how the door had been put together so he could take it apart. Because of jobs like this one, John has become quite skilled with tools. The more your son uses tools, the better suited he will be to take care of a future home.

## Earning Money

It is easy to forget the special feeling a young boy experiences by having his own money in his pocket. I once met a wise caretaker for the elderly who understood this principle well. She always made sure that the male residents had change in their pockets. I marveled at her insight as well as her love for the people she served.

Our sons also need to be able to earn some of their own money. They should "taste" the fruits of their labor. "He that laboureth laboureth for himself; for his mouth craveth it of him" (Proverbs 16:26).

When Joseph and John were this age, they earned money, and saved it, to buy nicer bicycles. In our family, we give our children their first bicycles as a gift, but they buy future bikes. Joseph and John have a new appreciation for how much work is required to earn enough money to buy an item they want. They also take greater pleasure in their bicycles since they purchased them with their own money. Lately, they have been asking to set up a savings account so they can begin saving for their houses like Nathan and Christopher.

## Schoolwork

Schoolwork is obviously instrumental in preparing your son for his future as a provider for his family. School has many benefits that you will want to keep in mind so that your son will gain as much as possible from his school time.

Obviously, the education he receives from his schooling is vital to him having marketable skills. Frequently these days, we hear news reports on the number of high school graduates who are illiterate. Illiteracy will certainly limit a man's potential for earning a livable wage. You want a son who is comfortable with reading, spelling, writing, and math skills. In addition, you would like for him to have a basic knowledge of many other disciplines such as history, science, health, art, music, government, and economics. You have many years to instill this fundamental information into your sons, but don't lose sight of the fact that school is a necessary part of preparing a son.

Sometimes a mom feels guilty if her children are not having "fun" in school. A homeschooling mom may feel it is her fault if her children have any negative attitudes toward their schoolwork.

She may think the children's complaining is because she didn't make school interesting or exciting enough.

Consider what happens when a child has a portion of his schoolwork that is especially challenging or even boring. That child has the opportunity to develop character that will be needed when he faces the same characteristics—challenging or boring—in a work environment. If the child complains about the schoolwork being difficult or boring and Mom allows the child to stop doing the schoolwork, what has been taught? Complaining and bad attitudes net a result the child wants!

On the other hand, if Mom encourages a child to persevere through hard assignments or ones that lack luster, she is teaching her child to face his future work with an attitude of diligence, determination, and responsibility. These opportunities to build character in a child through schoolwork will be present throughout the school years. It is likely the lessons to be learned will not be fully mastered even in the elementary years. However, it is possible to continue working toward the goal of positive attitudes concerning all schoolwork, no matter what it is.

I am not suggesting a child be forced to do schoolwork he is not capable of, nor am I recommending purposefully finding tedious schoolwork. We do want to encourage you, though, in following the curriculum path the Lord has directed you along. Even if some of the work generates negative responses from your children, use it for their good, but don't change your course because of it. Only rechart your school curricula direction at the leading of the Lord.

Learning to type is a skill you should schedule into your child's school time. No matter what vocation he goes into as an adult, it is likely he will need to know how to type. In most businesses, there are memorandums, sales orders, and business letters to generate, while much company interaction is via e-mail. Even if your son's future job requires no typing skills, daily life has come to revolve so greatly around e-mail and the Internet that he will find typing an immense help and time saver during his hours at home.

If it is obvious your son already has a bent and leading from the Lord toward a particular vocation, you can also begin at this age to allow some school time for him to pursue appropriate studies in that direction. Not only does this begin his education specifically applicable to his future, but it also helps discern whether this is really a viable career direction for him. Even if you don't have an indication of your son's future work, you can use school time to help you toward this discernment. For example, schedule computer time. Does he like it? Does he have an aptitude for it? What about shop time? Can he build a project? Does he enjoy working with his hands? Perhaps you will plan a foreign language into your son's school day. Does he have a natural ability to learn a foreign language? Is it exciting for him?

Use your son's school hours to prepare him to provide for a single-income family. Help him with character and attitudes that will support a good work ethic as an adult. Schedule some school that can help begin to discern his future vocational direction.

## Creative Toys

When you give your son toys, make sure they are good, creative toys that will provide wholesome learning experiences. Just because a product is called a toy, that doesn't mean it is something your child should play with. A toy is a vehicle for a child's imagination. It is a transport to new horizons of excitement. Therefore, beware of where your child is going. Be careful what your child is pretending. "Finally, brethren, whatsoever things are true, whatsoever things *are* honest, whatsoever things *are* just, whatsoever things *are* pure, whatsoever things *are* lovely, whatsoever things *are* of good report; if *there be* any virtue, and if *there be* any praise, think on these things" (Philippians 4:8). It is very important what goes into our children's minds.

When a wicked toy is given to a child, you are allowing your son to fill his mind with wickedness. "For your obedience is come abroad unto all *men*. I am glad therefore on your behalf: but yet I would have you wise unto that which is good, and simple concerning evil" (Romans 16:19). Paul, by the Holy Spirit, said that we are to be innocent in our knowledge of evil.

Creative building toys can be a positive use of time as they can teach good construction concepts without a child even knowing it. The only caution I have is to avoid the evil themes that companies have now introduced. These new themes may make the toys more sellable to a generation who has filled their minds with harmful imaginations from TV, but they will do your son no good.

A boy in this age range will still want to play. That is why it is important that what he is playing with will benefit his future vocation.

## Computers

When Joseph was ten years old, we purchased the professional version of Delphi for him. It is an extremely powerful computer programming language. He spent many of his "free" hours learning to program. He had no instruction other than what he could dig out of the books we had. He still has a long way to go, but he has learned a tremendous amount already.

Do you think he would have been motivated to learn programming if we allowed games on our computers? Probably not! He would only have played with the games. Computers are tools that, if mastered, can be used to provide a handsome wage for a man.

If you allow your son to see computers as toys, he will be less motivated to use them productively. Likely, he will not want to invest the mental effort required to develop necessary computer skills. However, when computers are used properly, children soon discover the thrill of learning new things. Even when mental effort is required, it will be "fun" to them!

Joseph developed tremendous computer skills during this age range, and I was treated to a glimpse of them following his twelfth birthday. He had received a birthday present that was wrapped in homemade paper with drawings of some mountains on it, decorated with stickers. Joseph decided to be creative with his thank-you note for this gift. He began by scanning the gift's wrapping paper and then brought that scan into Photoshop. Photoshop is a high-level software that is the industry standard for graphics professionals. Joseph spends a fair amount of time using Photoshop. Joseph added snow to the mountains and made some embellishments to the decorations on the paper. These were slight changes that complemented what had already been done to make the original homemade gift wrap design. Joseph then wrote his thank-you letter using that wrapping paper as the background. I was pleased with his creativity and his knowledge of the software demonstrated through this "project."

With the increasing computer abilities of children this age, it is even more critical to protect them from the Internet filth. Don't ever trust them to stay where they are allowed on the Internet without supervision. Would you "trust" your son not to play with a loaded gun left on the table? Of course you wouldn't, because it isn't really a matter of trust, it is a matter of prudence. The same principle is important regarding the Internet. It is a tool and not a toy.

Internet surfing is another form of entertainment with the same pitfalls we discussed in the chapter on appetites. If you create an appetite for mindless surfing, your son will reap the consequences when he is expected to be a responsible, wage-earning adult.

Computers are here to stay, and your children must know how to use them. They will give your son years of learning opportunities. Computers are not an option; they are a necessity.

## Avoid Negative Appetites

This is the age range when the entertainment pull will increase in strength. To resist this force your son must be well anchored. You must have his heart and be able to look down the road toward his adulthood, seeing the consequences of what you will allow into his life now. You must think, sow ... reap, sow ... reap, sow ... reap. What you allow to be sowed into your child's life at this age will be reaped when he is older.

Much has already been said about negative appetites. Please take it to heart, and evaluate your decisions based upon God's Word and His direction. When baseball, soccer, basketball, and every other imaginable sport, club, and activity come knocking on your door, what will you do? Will you have your son's future interests in mind or his current pleasure? Will you seek God's best or man's best?

## Television

If you love your son and future grandchildren, eliminate TV viewing from your home. "By the time today's child reaches age 70, he or she will have spent approximately seven years watching

TV" (American Academy of Pediatrics study, 1990). One of the best heritages you can give your children is a disdain for TV.

## Moldable Years

These years are very important as you look toward your son becoming a teenager. Others will tell you to expect your children to rebel. The truth is that you will reap what you sow. If you sow bad appetites and cultivate laziness, you will reap sorrow during the teenage years. Sow a desire to enjoy working alongside his parents, and you will reap a son who brings you joy.

Your son needs to see the world as an endless serving opportunity and not a vast playground. The only way that will happen is if his heart comes to see the real needs of humanity around him. God has placed us here to serve Him by reaching a lost and dying world. He may call some sons to serve Him as missionaries or pastors, but the majority He doesn't. Most are called to be ambassadors for Christ while serving Him in the workplace. We are to make Christ known in all we do. There is no greater joy than being in fellowship with the Lord and serving Him. Why not introduce your son to that experience in these years?

## Questions

1. Have you developed in your sons the habit of daily Bible reading and prayer?

2. What is your vision for your family? For each of your sons?

3. How can you work toward instilling a desire in your son to do his best?

4. What kinds of chores are your sons doing? Is it time to add to their chore responsibilities?

5. What real work projects can you find for your sons to do with you and also on their own?

6. What kinds of jobs are you willing to pay your sons to do?

7. How is your son's schoolwork preparing him for the future?

8. Do your sons have creative toys? Are there toys you need to weed out?

9. How can you use your computer to develop marketable skills in your son? Does he know how to type?

10. Evaluate any negative appetites you have allowed in your son. What could you replace them with?

———————————

Throughout history, the goal of child rearing
has been to train children to be responsible,
mature adults. Quite frankly, adolescence
has never been marked by its maturity nor
productivity; therefore, the desire was to
shorten adolescence as much as possible.

*David Barton*

———————————

# Age Thirteen to Graduation

---

*It is good for a man that he bear the yoke in his youth.*
*Lamentations 3:27*

---

Now is the time to reap what you have sown during your son's younger years. You should be experiencing an ever-increasing fellowship with your son as he matures into a man. It can be a time of joy, reward, and challenge. How fulfilling to watch your teenage son grow in the Lord and in his vocational abilities!

The more time your son spends developing marketable, vocational skills, the less time, and money, he will be spending on pursuits that are not beneficial. Parents need to do all they can to facilitate their son's best use of time.

Which do you believe will be the best plan for your son's life: what everyone else is doing or what God directs? Your challenge is to stay the course God has shown you for that son. You want to be sure to keep his heart.

## Spiritually

At the beginning of this age range you have a budding man, and by the end a maturing man. He should be a man of God who loves his Lord. His habit and pleasure needs to be daily Bible reading and prayer. These must become his lifeline to the Lord for direction.

Your son's ability to discern how God's Word applies to life and making decisions is very important during this age. This will be instrumental in his adequacy at providing for his family. How will he develop proficiency in applying God's Word to decisions? Begin by continuing to give him time to study God's Word. That way he will be familiar enough with Scripture to know where to look for passages relating to different topics. Then when he is faced with a decision or a desire to do something, give him an assignment of finding and researching Scriptures that relate to the decision. Have him document his research and the decision reached, remembering the importance of prayer throughout the decision-making process.

You can also use this approach to help your son "practice" making Biblical decisions on situations he might face in the future, such as: What if your boss asked you to lie? Would it be proper for a married man to have lunch alone with a woman not his wife? What if the other woman were a sales representative, and it was strictly a business lunch? What if a woman coworker asked for help to save her marriage? Let him study God's Word on these issues as part of his training in applying Scripture to decision making. Not only will that skill be developed, but he will also be equipped with a Biblical basis for facing such situations if they ever arise. This will help him to see that the Bible can be applied to discerning God's direction.

How does an Army infantryman become skilled with his rifle? He practices using it! Therefore I would encourage you to find ways for your son to teach and preach in order to develop his Bible knowledge, presentation of salvation, and comfort level in front of an audience. "Study to shew thyself approved unto God, a workman that needeth not to be ashamed, rightly dividing the word of truth" (2 Timothy 2:15). Your son not only needs experience in researching and understanding God's Word, but also in presenting it. He should see purpose in what he has been reading. You want him to taste the thrill of sharing Christ and discover areas needing further study. In his preparation, have him concentrate on presenting how the passage can be applied to one's life. Over time your son will more readily see how Scripture applies to his life and decision making.

If you are not aware of preaching or teaching opportunities, ask the Lord where you and your son could share publicly. Our country is full of nursing homes with residents who are hungry for someone to spend time with them. What better use of time than to share God's Word with them? "Pure religion and undefiled before God and the Father is this, To visit the fatherless and widows in their affliction, *and* to keep himself unspotted from the world" (James 1:27). If the word "preaching" sounds too intimidating, call it a short devotional.

You can make your ministry at the nursing home a church-type service, as our family does, and include many of the children. Take turns with your son being the preacher or teacher. You share one week, and he can the next. If any of your children are learning to play an instrument, let him play while you or an older child leads the group in singing. It will be an incredible time of growth and service!

Be committed to preparing your son spiritually during these years. If you are, he should be mighty in spirit and able to boldly stand before others without fear. He will understand how God's Word can be applied to the situations of life!

## Character

Developing our children's character is a continuing process. They are first taught what is right, and over time will have opportunities to demonstrate their positive character. We can even look at a child's failures as having great value for their future role as a father and worker.

Years ago I was encouraged to have a scheduled time when I would meet privately with each of my children. I arbitrarily set twelve as the beginning age for these meetings. We have found right after church on Sunday, while lunch is being prepared, to be an excellent time. One by one I will have a private "meeting" with each of the older children. I have come to value this time highly, and to view our meetings as second only in importance to our family Bible reading.

Any topic is fair game for a meeting as long as it is discussed calmly, in a spirit of love. Most weeks I will ask a son how his quiet time is going, what struggles he is having, and if he is having trouble with his thoughts. If there are problems with his other siblings, these will be discussed. If there are character issues I've observed, I will bring these up. Seldom is there a negative reaction from my son as he receives the concerns from a loving daddy's heart. In addition, I ask my son whether I am doing anything that is causing him difficulty. Occasionally I will question him as to areas of hypocrisy in my life to which I'm blind. I absolutely love my meeting time with my children. Friend, I treasure those minutes!

Whatever you do, be sure that you are having a regular opportunity to meet with your children and help them along the "narrow" path. These years can be difficult for a young man as he matures, and we want to be there with him.

## Leadership

A man who knows how to lead will have skills that help him do well in his vocation. Whether God directs toward self-employment or outside employment, your son will use the qualities that make him a leader. If he has his own company, he must be able to lead his employees. If he works for a company, his ability to lead will be recognized and rewarded. The question then is how to turn your son into a leader.

A husband is called to be the leader of his home. He must lead his family while he follows Christ. "But I would have you know, that the head of every man is Christ; and the head of the woman *is* the man; and the head of Christ *is* God" (1 Corinthians 11:3). This verse shows us that a son cannot lead until he first learns to follow.

For your son to be a wise follower, you must continue to give diligence to keeping his heart. We want him to look to his father for guidance and desire to please him. If that father-son role is healthy, your son should have learned to follow.

Teri and I led a local homeschool group for ten years. It was an opportunity for us to serve as a family. However, we were pleasantly amazed at the leadership skills our children developed through the responsibilities they volunteered to undertake in helping us with the group. Let me share with you some specific examples in the hope that they will give you a vision for how your sons can develop their leadership skills through ministry responsibilities. Our children were happy to be a part of our homeschool group ministry and own areas of responsibilities. This enabled the children to manage a project with limited risk. The responsibilities were important and needed to be done; however, it was not a catastrophe if there were slight problems.

Each year Christopher organized the group's spelling bee. He oversaw it from beginning to end. He first had to locate and motivate the children to participate. Then, over time, he would check with the spellers to make sure they were working on their word lists. He recruited judges, a pronouncer, and a refreshment coordinator and made sure they each understood their role. He confirmed that the facilities were reserved and set up. Those of you who have overseen an event know there are other jobs that need to be managed as well, but you get the idea. All in all, it was an excellent chance for Christopher to lead.

Christopher, with Sarah's help, was also responsible for organizing the children's programs that were held during the parents' meetings. They had to plan every minute of the evening so that the children would spend their time productively. The goal was to teach the children material that was profitable and practical. Christopher and Sarah would recruit other young people to help. They worked through the details of the evening and often had an organizational meeting. The children's programs were an excellent opportunity to practice leadership while ministering to others.

It is exciting to see sons become leaders. I want to have confidence that my boys will be good leaders of their families and will be capable of leading in the work environment.

## Servanthood

Part of preparing a son to be the provider for a single-income family is teaching him to serve others with joy. Isn't that the essence of being a good employer, employee, and parent? God will give your family opportunities to serve, and you can be sure He will grow your children through the experiences.

Don't be surprised if volunteer work leads to beneficial vocational skills. Nathan, at age fourteen, began to serve the home-school group by laying out the newsletter. Originally we used WordPerfect, then Word, and finally Quark. Producing the home-school newsletter was incredible experience and gave him a reason to learn more about each respective computer program.

Nathan's expertise with WordPerfect led to an offer to become a system operator for WordPerfect's support bulletin board, where he would answer WordPerfect users' questions. That, in turn, led to him receiving a letter of recommendation from WordPerfect Corporation, which was instrumental in his being hired to teach WordPerfect classes to local Army officers. All of that vocational training grew from a willingness to serve!

God desires godly seed, equipped as men and women of God. He will give your family opportunities to serve others. Confirm that God is opening the door, then enter through as a family. Expect your son to become a valued servant at work and at home.

## A Vision

It is important that you keep a vision before your son. What goals has God led you to for him? Will he be purchasing a house or vehicle debt free? Does he desire to be a man of God? Maybe God is leading him to start a business. Whatever it is, be sure he has purpose in life consistent with God's leading.

During this age our sons came to own the goal of purchasing a house debt free before marriage. This goal made it easier for them to save their money and reduced the temptation to spend it. Their goal gave them real purpose for work as well.

An underlying part of our vision for our children must be to make Christ known in all we do. That is when a Christian's life is really meaningful. "To whom God would make known what *is* the riches of the glory of this mystery among the Gentiles; which is Christ in you, the hope of glory: Whom we preach, warning every man, and teaching every man in all wisdom; that we may present every man perfect in Christ Jesus: Whereunto I also labour, striving according to his working, which worketh in me mightily" (Colossians 1:27-29). A paycheck lasts a moment. However, real, meaningful work of eternal value is what is done in the human heart when Jesus Christ regenerates a person. May we never be so focused on work that we lose sight of the work He did for all mankind. Life aside from Christ is meaningless.

## Even More Work and Less Play

The Lord has "wired" men to work: unfortunately, the entertaining, fun things of this world can drown out that desire. How to keep your son working productively and away from the pleasures of this world is a challenge for you as the parent. "I pray not that thou shouldest take them out of the world, but that thou shouldest keep them from the evil. They are not of the world, even as I am not of the world" (John 17:15-16).

One excellent way to stir the desire for working is by helping your son start a business. Remember Eric? Even though he was not learning programming as his father wanted, he still benefited greatly from his start-up graphics design business. By staying busy, Eric did not have the time or the desire to "hang around with the guys." For two years, he poured his heart into making his business successful.

Leading your son toward more work and less play may mean providing him with necessary work tools. When Joseph was twelve, he was progressing well in programming, web page layout, and graphic design. Unfortunately, we did not have a computer available as often as he needed it. So we found a refurbished, name-brand system that was very inexpensive, but quite powerful. Then Joseph had his "own" system and was able to spend more time on the projects that challenged him. Parents should be willing to invest financially in sons, if necessary.

If God leads your son toward automotive work, you might look for an old car he can work on. If woodwork holds vocational interest, acquire some equipment and let your son do some projects. This could easily lead to a business for him.

Wherever the Lord leads, pursue it! In a year's time, many parents will spend a significant amount of money on sporting activities and equipment for their sons. Why not invest that money in something worthwhile? If God is leading in a particular direction, He will provide the funds or equipment that is necessary for your son to learn.

## Vocational Skills

Vocational skills usually become a focus after high school either in the form of college, trade school, or apprenticeship. Unfortunately, by that time, several prime years of learning have been lost. It is important to realize the significance of making every minute count during high school. The more marketable skills your son has when he graduates from high school, the more versatile he will be as a worker in our competitive world. You will want to invest time, energy, and money to begin vocationally equipping your son. By now you have probably noticed your son's particular vocational aptitudes and interests. Pursue them! This will be a tremendously positive use of his time to be working on these skills.

Billy, a sixteen-year-old, has been helping a young man who owns his own service business. Billy is not able to work full time because of school, but with the hours he is putting in, he is gaining significant experience in this trade. By the time he graduates from high school, he will know if this is something he wants to pursue full time.

Troy chose to attend college. The vocational skills he learned during his high school years enabled him to have a high-paying contract job while he attended college. If young people would concentrate on learning marketable skills at this age instead of majoring in entertainment, many would not have to borrow for college, a vehicle, or a house.

By the time my second-born son was fifteen, we had noticed his aptitude for numbers, finances, and accounting. When he was sixteen, he worked a full tax season for a certified public accountant. As a result of this time, Christopher learned much, but he was also able to see that it was not God's direction for him to become a CPA. Instead, the bookkeeping and accounting he learned during that tax season have become skills he uses in our business, but they are not his full-time employment.

We have purposed that our sons have as many marketable skills as possible. At the ages of twenty-four and twenty-two, they had acquired the following combined, well-paid experience: owning their own business, professional photography, website design, digital imaging, professional level layout and design for electronic or printed display, business accounting, sales, network design, Microsoft Certified Systems Engineer, Novell Certified Engineer, computer network administration, computer hardware repair, book publishing, book writing, technical writing, and teaching experience for Word, Excel, WordPerfect, and QuickBooks. I left out areas where they have minimal skills, as well as their annuity and servant related skills.

What about a young man who is waiting for God to give him direction for life? What should he do if God hasn't shown him what to do vocationally? Does he not prepare for any work until the Lord shows him exactly what his life's work is to be? I encourage a son in these circumstances to learn as many possible marketable skills he can under his father's direction. At best, when God's leading comes, he will be equipped to begin his vocation right away. At worst, he will have extra skills; who knows when and how the Lord may use them. Therefore, keep your son busy learning!

Vocational experience is like rolling a snowball downhill: the more vocational experience your son has, the better he will be at what he does. Friend, if you want to prepare your son for a vocation, give him all the responsibility and experience he can handle. He should be well equipped for life.

## Computer Skills

Part of the vocational training necessary for any young man is computer expertise. Many jobs require some level of computer usage these days. Even a carpenter may find himself using the word processor to correspond with suppliers and customers, a financial software package to keep his books, and a spreadsheet to track inventory!

By this age your son should be an excellent typist. Now he can become proficient in more advanced use of a computer. He needs to know the computer's general architecture and what its various components do. You want to have him install and remove programs and not be afraid to troubleshoot a family member's computer problem. Notice I didn't say he could always solve the problem. However, it is advantageous that he be willing to try to figure out what is wrong.

You will want to find computer application projects that require him to learn more. A spreadsheet is a very common business application, but you will need to work to come up with practical projects for him to use what he is learning. If he has his own business, there will be data from the business that he can use in a spreadsheet. We learn by doing. Your job is to find computer projects that will cause him to grow.

You might begin with an inexpensive, generic home office software package. After he has mastered the word processor, spreadsheet, and database, it will be time to purchase a professional business office package. This may be a significant expense, but it will pay dividends for his lifetime. Pray that God will allow your expenditures to be revenue producing. Then your son will be able to finance his own learning experiences.

What will you do when your son runs into difficulties learning or using a software program? Will you let him quit in frustration? No! Encourage him to persevere, with Dad right beside him. Go to the library, and check out books. Use the web for research.

Even if your son's future job doesn't require computer experience, his computer knowledge will benefit him in his personal life. For example, I can type at least twice as fast as I can write, and I am able to read it when I'm finished! I come close to "loving" my Bible software program. In a fraction of the time it used to take, I can research Biblical words and references. These computer tools are invaluable to me in my writing and speaking.

As a provider for his family, your son should know how to track his finances. The home finance software packages make this very easy, and he needs to be familiar with one. In fact, tracking his finances would be a good habit for him to acquire as he begins earning money. This will help him manage the money the Lord provides.

Friend, computers are here to stay. Consider what computer skills and tools can mean to your son in his daily life or even his vocation. The level of skill to which you challenge your son will depend on whether a computer will be a vital part of his vocation or simply a timesaving device in his daily life.

## Beginning a Business

America is the land of opportunity, and those opportunities are available to your son. One option that will provide him with incredible experience and learning is to start a business. Whether he continues his business after high school or simply uses it as a vehicle for learning, it certainly could benefit him.

Nathan and Christopher began a lawn mowing business when they were ages thirteen and eleven. Maxwell's Mowing Service was an excellent source of income and experience for them. To ensure there was positive growth for the boys through their business, Teri and I gave oversight as needed. We had a voice in business decisions and also acted behind the scenes to provide quality control.

It would be worthwhile to list some of the benefits our sons experienced. The boys learned to work hard under physically difficult circumstances, as summers in Kansas are hot and muggy! They learned to manage money and perform business accounting. They acquired customer service skills. If their business was to succeed, they had to do their best. Within a couple of years, the boys were averaging fifteen dollars per hour each, allowing them to save a significant amount of money. They learned the importance of maintaining their equipment. They had to manage their time and spend it wisely. They were able to set their own schedule consistent with the needs of the family. They were never bored. They had good fellowship and avoided evil companions. They also developed a reputation throughout the neighborhood as hardworking, honest young men. A young man's business can be of tremendous profit, and not just financially.

Here are a few more benefits of beginning a business. Your son will learn how to research the local ordinances pertaining to a business in a home, which tax laws are applicable, how to complete tax documentation, how to acquire a federal tax ID, how to use accounting software, introductory marketing skills, customer service skills, and—maybe the most important—how to begin another business should God lead in a different direction in the future.

Christopher has been involved in creating two family-owned corporations. When he wanted to begin a photography business on the side, it was straightforward for him to do the research and fill out all of the federal—and state—required paperwork. He had done it twice before!

Your son's business could allow him to save enough money to pay for higher education, bankroll another start-up company, or have a handsome beginning toward a debt-free house. Even if his business flops financially, it is okay as long as his attitude is right and he learns from his mistakes. Business success or failure—either way—he wins.

## Outside Employment

I have often spoken to a father of a sixteen-year-old son who has just started a job. The father may or may not be excited about what the son is doing, but he is usually glad his son is working.

I applaud the son's industry, but can be grieved when I learn where the son is employed. Please exercise caution, with much thought and prayer, before allowing your son to work outside the home.

The main advantage of a son being employed is the availability of immediate skills that he learns and can further apply. He is able to glean from others' experience and sample different jobs to see what he might be particularly suited for.

The disadvantages of outside employment, if they are present, can offset all the advantages to include his paycheck. The pay is frequently far less than what this teen could earn from his own business. His boss dictates the hours the son works. He can be exposed to significant worldly influences and temptations. It is possible that the worst negative would be for his heart to turn toward his boss or a coworker. Work circumstances have even been known to lead to an immoral relationship at this vulnerable age.

Sometimes a father will say his son is working for a wonderful, Christian man in a Christian business. Yes, but it still is likely he will be working with non-Christians. If your son were in this situation, you would want to visit the company on a regular basis to verify that your expectations of a Christian environment are being met. I have been quite surprised at what I've observed in "Christian" businesses. Remember, just because it is Christian owned and operated does not mean it is a place you want your son to work.

If you choose to let your son work outside the home, visit him often at the job. Make it a condition, with his employer, of his working there. Know whom he is working with, and make sure he is learning beneficial skills. If he isn't learning, he probably shouldn't be working there. These are critical years in developing life skills, and time cannot be wasted for a paycheck alone. If you sense his heart is drifting away from you even slightly, he needs to quit. Parents, you are responsible before God for this son; be zealous for God's best in his life.

## Annuity Skills

Let me define what I mean by annuity skills. These are skills a young man can acquire to save him from having to hire another to perform the task. These skills would include landscaping, painting, carpentry, sheet rocking, plumbing, auto mechanics, and masonry. Think of how much money your son could save over the course of a lifetime if he had some skills in each of these areas or was at least willing to find a book to help him learn how to attack the project.

I have met many men through the years who say they aren't "handy" around the home. They often go on to justify this by saying they never learned any of those skills from their father.

Wait a minute! That is no excuse—especially for homeschooling dads! Homeschooling moms are expected to teach material that may be totally new to them each year. If we request that of the moms, shouldn't dads be able to lead the way regarding teaching our sons annuity skills?

When we purchased the house we currently live in, it only had three bedrooms. As our family grew from four to eight children while in this house, we needed more bedrooms. We decided to convert much of the unfinished basement space into bedrooms. Nathan and Christopher were in this chapter's age range at that time and worked with me on the remodeling project. I loved working with them! Not only was it excellent father-son time, but they also learned several annuity skills. Now that Nathan has his own home, he has been able to undertake many repair and remodeling jobs.

Computer know-how is an additional area I have come to view as an annuity skill. Nathan and Christopher do much to support the computers we have in our home. Since computers are the major tools of our business, we are constantly having computer issues that need to be addressed. If we had to pay someone each time we had a computer system reloaded, the network rewired, or a reconfiguration, we would be paying out a significant sum of money.

There is a wealth of books and materials available to guide you through learning these skills. Help your son seek the information he needs for the task at hand if he doesn't already know how to do it. Begin while he is young, and be determined that he will have a handsome portfolio of annuity skills by the time he is ready to leave your home. He will likely bless you for it!

## Projects

Assigning your son projects will continue to be a valuable tool for training him. His days can be filled with one meaningful project after another.

It will now be good to give him an occasional project that is clearly beyond his current skill level. Make it difficult enough that, in order to complete it, his "brain will sweat." He needs to be challenged to the point of wanting to quit. He must know how to face a difficult problem, something he considers impossible, and learn that he can conquer it.

This is an important milestone for each child and is one of the biggest benefits of a good college. It appears that a person who will succeed in his work must be able to successfully complete a difficult assignment with a cheerful, persevering attitude. That comes with practice, and you can either assist your son in this area or pay someone else handsomely to do it.

A homeschooling mother might warn you that your child will respond differently to you than he will to someone else. Your child will not likely demonstrate visible anger toward an instructor, but he may openly vent great frustration toward you. This provides both of you with a learning opportunity. Will you be calm if he is angry or frustrated? Can you help him work through those negative emotions and encourage him to patiently continue on? Will you be able to give him subtle direction and hints without telling him how to do it?

An important aspect of assigning projects is including a deadline. Think about it: a deadline makes the difference between a stroll in the park and a sprint. Your son will feel some real pressure if he has a date by which the project must be completed. Perhaps you could offer a reward, such as dinner out with Dad, if the project is successfully accomplished on time.

The underlying principle of your involvement in this type of project should be to provide your son guidance with a spirit of gentleness. If you can't avoid harshness, don't give your son these kinds of challenging projects.

Projects are an excellent tool that can be skillfully used to hone your son. Watch his heart carefully while you challenge him, but don't exasperate him. "And, ye fathers, provoke not your children to wrath: but bring them up in the nurture and admonition of the LORD" (Ephesians 6:4).

Cheer him on to complete each task with a dependence on His Lord. He will find that prayer needs to be an integral part of any difficulty a person faces.

## Schoolwork

A son's schoolwork might be what many would consider the most important part of preparing that son to be able to provide for a single-income family. Without a doubt, it will be foremost on any homeschooling mother's mind! Mom is pouring herself into teaching these children. She wants to know it is for their good!

So what about his schoolwork? What effect does it have on a boy's ability to eventually be a working adult? I expect there are a multitude of educational experts out there who would love to answer that question. However, I would encourage you to consider a few things with me, all the while looking to God's leading. Be encouraged, dear parent, that God has a plan for your son, and you are the ones He will hold accountable to follow it. Please take what anyone says and pass it by your Lord to determine if that is His will for your son.

These are the years in which you are diligently seeking the Lord for your son's vocational future. Design your school curricula accordingly, keeping in mind your state laws. While you might not be certain, at this point, of the specific direction your son will take after high school, you still need to formulate school plans based on the possibilities the Lord has placed on your hearts.

If you know your son is headed for college, you will want your son's high school courses geared toward college prep. You will have to spend time researching entrance requirements to potential schools your son might attend. Don't wait until he is a junior in high school to do this. Do it before he even enters high school so you can plan his course of study to meet, and perhaps exceed, the university's entrance requirements!

This would be a good time to check out scholarship criteria since this may affect the courses your son takes. We know a family whose son qualified for excellent academic scholarships. When his university ranked the top academic students to determine the amount of scholarship money each would receive, the basic academic courses and test scores were so close that the school rated highest the students who had four years of a foreign language. Information like this can be very helpful in planning your son's high school courses.

Particularly if college is any possibility for your son, it would be good to look into setting up a record-keeping system to create a high school transcript. You can even give this project to your son. However, if you wait until he is applying to universities to generate a transcript, you will likely be extremely frustrated. What you thought you would never forget about his freshman courses may be hard to recall several years later.

These are the years to allow as much school time as possible for developing skills that will be directly useful in a business or vocation. Even if your son is headed for college, you still want to do this. Think about how a son with business and vocational skills can help to support himself through college!

For example, purchase an accounting software program and a tutorial book to go with it. Design a high school-level course so that your son learns how to use an accounting program and set up bookkeeping for a real or made-up business. Allow him school time to complete this course. Then your son will be equipped, through his schoolwork, to take care of the accounting aspect of his business.

A school course learning to make a brochure—something almost every business needs—could develop more business skills. Purchase a computer program and accompanying book that will allow your son to design brochures. Schedule school time for him to learn this program. As a final project, he could even design a brochure for a real company—just ask around!

Courses could be developed for just about any interest. Working models of car engines are available. First he could build the model, and then he could write a paper about how it works. Next he could research air conditioning technology. Go to a junk-yard and purchase the components of the system. Bring them home and reassemble them into a simulated working system. Finally, take each piece apart and have him describe how it works. In a similar fashion, courses for other interests can be developed.

Work together with your son in making his high school curriculum decisions. Encourage him to seek the Lord, along with you, concerning how these hours can be most profitably spent. Communicate frequently with your son so that you know his interests, and observe him so that you know his talents. Take these into consideration as you plan with your son his high school direction.

When our oldest sons were in high school, the Lord was not directing them to college. Therefore, we encouraged them to study math only through algebra II, using further math course time for computer study instead. They were seeing God's leading them into having their own computer-related business. The computer courses would be necessary for their vocations; calculus might not. If at some point the Lord showed them a change of vocational course that needed higher math, they could always study it at that point.

God has a plan for your son, but you are the ones He will hold accountable for following it. Don't be blown off course by the latest educational frenzy that everyone loves. Take what anyone says and pass it by your Lord to determine if that is His will for your son.

## Training Prior to Graduation

The possibilities for preparing a teenage son to provide for his future family are almost limitless. Praying for and seeking out the opportunities and direction the Lord has for your son is critical. You want his hours to be profitably occupied through learning, working, and serving. Each of these areas holds great potential for developing your son's portfolio of qualifications to live on a single income.

A parent's investment of time in a son cannot be overstated. Dads and moms are still highly needed through these years. You will have the wisdom to help your son make decisions on educational, work, and ministry options. Your prayer support is invaluable. Investing in the tools your son needs to begin a business may be a part of preparing your son for his future jobs.

Have you caught a vision for how productive the years from thirteen through high school graduation can be? Will you be committed to helping your son discover God's best through these years?

## Questions

1.  Discuss some possible assignments you could give your son to relate decision making to Scripture. What are some scenarios you would like to have him research?

2.  What vocational skills do you think are important for your son?

3.  What computer skills would you like your son to master?

4.  Are there opportunities in your son's life to develop leadership skills? If so, what are they?

5.  Is your son involved in serving? How?

6.  What specifically are you doing to help develop positive character traits in your son?

7.  What steps would you need to take to facilitate your son starting a business?

8.  What projects would you like to see your son undertake?

9.  What visions do you want to instill in your son?

10. How can you design your son's schoolwork to help him be prepared for his vocation?

11. What annuity skills should your son learn? How will this be accomplished?

---

Today, for whatever reason, we
attempt to prolong adolescence and
unfortunately embed the tendencies
of adolescence in the adult (decisions
made based on what is fun or enjoyable
rather than what is right; the world
revolving around the individual child; etc.).
Consequently, we have far too many adults
who still act like adolescents, displaying
their selfishness and immaturity in public
office, in professional sports, in media, in
marriage, and every other arena.

*David Barton*

---

# Post High School

---

*Man goeth forth unto his work and to
his labour until the evening.*
*Psalm 104:23*

---

Some parents wait until their son has graduated from high school to begin seriously preparing him for a career. Others have been developing their sons vocationally for years.

If you have only recently begun to consider this subject, there is much to do. It will be difficult to attain what you might have if you had started sooner, but not impossible! Begin by rereading this book beginning at Chapter Six. Be confident that you are building upon a sure foundation. Then proceed gradually to apply the suggestions in each chapter. Proceed to the next chapter only after you are satisfied with the progress your son has made through the suggestions in the current chapter. Be committed that if it takes your son until he is in his twenties to have him properly prepared, you will do it.

For those parents who have been preparing their son for years, be encouraged that the fruits of your labor are close to being harvested. You may decide that your son is to continue with his education and training. Or there may be other plans. Possibly he owns a business or is about to begin employment with another company. Regardless of the direction, be sure of God's leading.

## Spiritually

Your son should be well grounded in the Word, able to make wise decisions, and a man of God. If not, then that should be your top priority. When is spiritual grounding complete? My recommendation would be that as long as your son is under your roof, strive to encourage him spiritually. Isn't that what a brother in Christ is supposed to do? "Iron sharpeneth iron; so a man sharpeneth the countenance of his friend" (Proverbs 27:17).

There are undoubtedly many workingmen who are not mature believers, but as the examples in Chapter One illustrate, there are consequences. Even if your son goes on to receive an advanced degree, if he lacks the ability to make wise, Biblical decisions, there is no guarantee he will ever earn enough income to adequately provide for his family.

Herb, from Chapter One, is a good example of a very nice person earning a tremendous salary, but who was unable to make wise decisions and wound up in serious debt. If he were to experience a reduction in his salary before being able to sell his elaborate home, he could lose everything! He freely admits that it wasn't God's will for him to purchase that house.

May we do all we can to spiritually prepare our sons. When they are men of God seeking to please their Lord, they will be in His hands—and there is nowhere else I'd rather have them be!

## Serving

"And whosoever of you will be the chiefest, shall be servant of all. For even the Son of man came not to be ministered unto, but to minister, and to give his life a ransom for many" (Mark 10:44-45). We are on earth to serve others, not ourselves. Is your son serving others? Hopefully, by now he has acquired an appetite for serving.

The church is rich with opportunities for young men to serve. In fact, it may even gobble up all of your son's available serving time. We must keep in mind that Jesus served both in and out of the temple. That is a good example for us. We are to let our light shine for the world to see. The world will not see our light shining if it only shines inside the church.

For example, several post–high school young adults from our church minister at a local housing authority. They work with the children from the complex in a weekly after-school program. Jesus is proclaimed and deep friendships between the children who attend the program and the leaders are developed.

Another example of serving in the post–high school years is Christopher. He helps his grandfather with a Living Last Supper performance each year near Resurrection Sunday. He is responsible for the lights, staging, sound, setup, and teardown. There are a lot of details to manage, including overseeing his assistants during the performance. It takes a significant amount of his time each year, but he loves to help.

When serving others is our joy, we have the opportunity of a lifetime of joy. When our joy is in our entertainment, our joy is limited by our income.

## Visions Fulfilled

This can be an exciting time to watch God fulfill the visions that He has given your son. These may include a young man's successful business, completing a course of study, certifications, degrees, or even purchasing a vehicle or home debt free.

Is the ability to purchase a home debt free a good goal for sons? Think about what a burden rent or mortgage payments are. They pressure men to work in places where Christians should not be employed. I have also known men, under tremendous financial pressure due to their mortgage, who participated in unethical and illegal business dealings. Concern over loss of income should never hold a Christian to a job with which his Lord would not be pleased.

Now can you see why we have presented our children with this goal of a debt-free house? Many parents may see saving for a house as unrealistic because a mortgage payment has hounded them throughout their marriage. However, I would encourage you to ask the Lord if it might not be a worthy goal for your sons.

Teri and I would have loved to provide our children with homes according to Proverbs 19:14, "House and riches *are* the inheritance of fathers: and a prudent wife *is* from the LORD." Unfortunately, we are nowhere near being able to do that. However, we can provide them with room and board for as long as it takes them to save up for their house. Even then it is our desire that they would continue to live with us until God provides them a spouse.

If a young man has prepared well during high school, he should fairly easily be able to earn thirty-five thousand dollars or more a year when he graduates. Start with a yearly income and then subtract tithes, offerings, and taxes. Then money must be put aside for transportation, insurance (medical and auto), and other incidental expenses. If your son is frugal, he should be able to save 50 percent or slightly more of his income while living at home.

Within six years from high school graduation, your twenty-four-year old son will have saved one hundred thousand dollars, not counting any appreciable interest. I find that very exciting. If he earned less than thirty-five thousand a year, it just means he must save a little longer.

Depending upon the location, size, and age of the house your son will purchase, he might not even need one hundred thousand.

There are so many possibilities and intriguing options, but nothing happens unless a son has a vision, and you help him prepare.

My sons have found that as they accumulate a significant amount of savings, the interest starts to really add up. This has given them a real appreciation for earning, rather than paying, interest. That is where the battle is won! When you are successful in motivating toward a goal, your sons will own that goal and work toward achieving it.

I want to encourage you with the possibilities for your own son. If a father says, "My son isn't involved with computers and can't make that much money," my question for him is, "Do you think your son could learn to handle a commercial lawn mower?" I think you will agree that most sons are capable of running a lawn mower.

Mark, a recent high school graduate, has his own lawn mowing business. It is nothing fancy, just one man with a commercial, walk-behind mower. I just spoke with him on his mobile phone as he was about to start on another lawn. I asked him if he thought a young man could clear thirty-five thousand a year by mowing lawns. He chuckled and said, "Yes, pretty easily in fact!" Then he pointed out that income came from mowing lawns for only five months, during the growing season.

The God-given visions your son has for his future are instrumental in placing positive goals before him. Encourage that son in working toward these goals. They will be beneficial in his striving to be prepared to support a single-income family.

## Further Education

Whether your son continues his education—and, if so, where he goes—may be one of the biggest decisions of his life. Schools are described as learning institutions. A student sitting under a professor's teaching will be influenced by that professor's words and attitudes. If the school is a secular institution, your son could adopt that worldview or at the very least be influenced by it. The university he attends, could potentially impact every decision he makes after having attended that school.

I used to listen to a popular conservative radio talk show. I thought the host's mockery of the President and constant sexual innuendoes were wrong, but I felt the program to be a good source for political information. I purposed just to ignore the bad and receive the good.

However, I was surprised to discover that even though my intention was to filter out the negative content, it still had an impact on my attitudes. I began struggling with impure thoughts, and I was unable to shake them until I quit listening to the program. Could your son be similarly influenced by teaching, discussion, and the worldview at his university?

If you choose to send your son on for more education, I would implore you to be zealous in your evaluation of the school and your son's maturity. Instead of the godly influence of his parents, peers and professors will now surround him. That is why you want to carefully evaluate your son's maturity, the school, and God's direction where higher education is concerned.

Years ago there was a common saying in corporate Informational Technology (IT) departments. These IT departments were responsible for purchasing and maintaining the company's large computer systems. The saying went like this, "No one was ever fired for buying IBM." That generic statement meant the IT manager who purchased IBM computer equipment would not lose his job, even if the installation and resulting system were terrible. In essence, this manager couldn't be blamed if there were future computer problems because he had followed the example of other IT managers. Obviously he'd made the right decision. Therefore, if something happened to go wrong, it was an unavoidable problem that could be blamed on no one.

Still there were many computer installations where the IT manager made that popular choice, yet the system was an absolute failure! Some flopped because of the manager's poor planning and implementation. Others bombed because of the computer company he was relying on. Sometimes the purchases were an extreme waste of time and money because the company did not need the system.

There were also many companies that did have success stories. Those companies had a real need. Then, because of proper planning and installation, they ended up with a system that worked beautifully for them.

I think the IT buying situation is analogous to the current higher education climate. Sending a child to college is the accepted norm. It is assumed that as long as parents put their son in college, they have made the best decision for him.

Unfortunately, if God isn't directing your son to attend higher education and you encourage him to go, his life might never be the same. If God hasn't provided the finances, your son could carry the financial burden of repaying student loans for many years. Many young men meet their spouses at college. If your son isn't living in the center of God's will, how could that affect his consideration of a spouse? Other wrong influences may negatively affect his walk with the Lord and his relationship with you. All of these can have a potential damaging impact on your son's provision for a single-income family. That is why I encourage you to be certain higher education is God's will.

The issue of continuing education can be condensed down to this: always strive for God's best and do not settle for anything less. If God says do it, then you must. If God says don't, then regardless of what others are doing, don't. "For what is a man profited, if he shall gain the whole world, and lose his own soul? or what shall a man give in exchange for his soul?" (Matthew 16:26).

## Vocational Skills

Much has already been said about developing marketable skills. If the skills have not been developed, then go back and read the two previous chapters. If you and your son have been working together to prepare for his future, you will probably have discerned God's leading for his vocation by now.

Once that direction has been made clear, work at further developing that area of expertise. However, don't jump at every chance to have someone train your son. All the previous cautions still apply to outside training. When God directs, He will use the training opportunities for His glory. If He doesn't direct, then stay clear of them.

Training is often a high-priced commodity, and if your son is able to study on his own, he can save thousands of dollars. For example, we agreed with Nathan that God was leading him to pursue further certification. To learn the necessary material he could either take classes or buy the curriculum and study independently. Nathan chose to study on his own even though he knew it would take significantly longer to get his certification. He was successful in achieving his certification and saved himself thousands of dollars.

Are you able to see how you can help your son in more ways than simply writing a tuition check? If you will invest in preparing him through the years, he will reap rewards his entire life.

## Bearing Fruit

Even through the post–high school years, there will still be vocational and educational decisions to be made. You want to be constantly in an attitude of prayer, along with your son, concerning each of these decisions. Try to resist making a decision along the lines of what others are doing, just because it is popular. You will have no regrets or concerns whether decisions were chosen correctly as long as you have confidence that they were in accordance with God's directions.

If your son has acquired a variety of vocational skills, it should become obvious which direction the Lord is leading for a life's work. Endeavor to expand that area of skill and experience to confirm the direction.

Continue to encourage your son in the Lord. Godly fathers and mothers desire that their sons live for the Lord. With gentleness, "let us consider one another to provoke unto love and to good works" (Hebrews 10:24). Most sons are driving by this age and are able to serve and minister beyond the immediate neighborhood. Serving others is a great way to fellowship and should be a natural part of his life.

Post high school is the time when you will see your son fully functioning as a man. He will be pursuing a vocation, working in his business, or attending higher education. While he may not yet have a family to support, you want him to be prepared for that possibility when the time comes. The investments of time and effort you have made through your son's childhood should now be paying dividends!

## Questions

1. Think back and discuss the preparations you want to have in place in your son's life by this age toward his ability to support his family.

2. On what will you base your decision regarding whether your son pursues a higher education?

3. What spiritual factors do you view to be key in your son as a post–high school graduate that will have the most influence on his providing for a single-income family?

4. If your son is not yet to this age, have you begun to observe vocational interests and attitudes? What are they? Have you started praying about them?

5. What kind of serving opportunities do you think would be beneficial at this age and contribute toward your son's maturity as a wage-earning adult?

———————————

I have observed that there seem to be two types
of individuals when it comes to work: those
who embrace hard work as a virtue, and
those who dislike it and try to avoid it.
*David Barton*

———————————

# Will He Be Prepared?

———————

*For thou shalt eat the labour of thine hands:*
*happy shalt thou be, and it shall be well with thee.*
*Psalm 128:2*

———————

I am convinced that even though the task of preparing a son to provide for a single-income family is daunting, it is one that parents should want to willingly embrace. Every parent desires that his adult son be able to function productively in the adult wage-earning world no matter what vocation the Lord calls him to. Even more so, many Christian parents want their son's wife able to be a full-time, stay-at-home mother. This necessitates the family living off one income. The ability of a son to productively work is the fruition of the years of investment a parent makes in his children.

## Work

The Lord has made clear to us that work is a part of a man's life. "Six days shalt thou labour, and do all thy work" (Exodus 20:9). "The labour of the righteous *tendeth* to life" (Proverbs 10:16). "Man goeth forth unto his work and to his labour until the evening" (Psalm 104:23). Therefore, as parents, it would seem wise that we be attentive to the impact we can have on our children during their formative years. Rather than a child growing up to shun work—putting up with it as a necessary evil—we want him to rejoice in his labor and find it to be good. ". . . for my heart rejoiced in all my labour . . ." (Ecclesiastes 2:10).

Instead of feeling like we are spoiling our son's childhood, how exciting it is to know the work we require of him and the work we do with him will build advantageous attitudes, character, and skills into his life. These are necessary qualities that will facilitate his ability to provide for his family. Remember that childhood is the training ground for adulthood. While children will naturally gravitate toward play, it is the parent's responsibility to gently direct them toward work.

## Too Great a Task?

The myriad of suggestions and ideas presented in this book may be overwhelming to some parents. That is certainly not my purpose. Rather, I want to give you as much information as I can so that you can prayerfully discern what will be helpful for your sons and what won't. Obviously, no one will be able to do what is written in these pages all at once. Your plan should be to build, stone upon stone, as you learn how to help your son prepare to provide for a family and then implement what you have learned. When one stone is in place and it becomes stable, you are ready for the next stone. Stone by stone, your foundation is laid for training a son to be a wage-earning adult.

There will be parents who estimate the time and cost of personal investment in the lives of their sons, as outlined here, to be high. These dads might be spending ten to twelve hours or more at their jobs, which leaves little, if any, time for their family. In these cases, the cost must be fully counted. Remember Bob from Chapter One? He traded work hours for the morality of his children. You may be forced to make a similar choice. Which will it be?

## Young Men of Today

I am concerned as I observe young men who are not equipped for the life in front of them. Perhaps they are living for all the pleasure and fun they can get now. Maybe they are wandering aimlessly, doing nothing while waiting for the Lord to drop their vocation into their lap. Some are jumping from one job to another hoping desperately to finally find the perfect work that "tickles their fancy" and pays handsomely.

I see the parents' role as crucial in helping their son avoid the scenarios just mentioned. This is not a task for the fainthearted, though. The path of least resistance is to do nothing purposeful and hope everything turns out fine. Judging from the young men I see these days, their vocational success might not be too difficult to predict.

I have also observed families who have implemented much of what you read in these pages. They have produced, in accordance with the Lord's direction, young men who are mature, responsible adults. With hearts turned toward fully following the Lord and serving others, these men are entering the work force as productive wage earners. They are able to support their families on one income. In addition, they are prepared to provide for their families by being the spiritual leader. They have character qualities to make them great husbands, fathers, and workers.

## The Parents

No matter what age your son, you can affect his future ability to support his family. Working purposefully according to his age level, you will want to invest as much as possible—particularly of yourself—in this long-term project. The Lord has given parents the responsibility to train their children (Proverbs 22:6).

The disciplines and character God has built into Dad and Mom's lives are crucial for producing a son prepared to enter the work force and succeed. Your example is perhaps more foundational than any other piece of your son's training. That modeling you do, sometimes without even being aware of it, will cement positive or negative attitudes in your son toward work.

## The Lord

You want to keep in mind your complete dependence on, and looking to, the Lord for direction as you are considering your present preparation for your son's future. He will give you ideas and counsel through your training stages. He will present opportunities for your sons to work alongside you. He will make serving opportunities available in the home, community, and outside ministries. He is the One who changes the heart of a reluctant worker, not to mention a father with areas of weakness in his own life. Each decision you make that will impact your son's future ability to support his family should be bathed in prayer.

No one is more concerned for your son than his Lord. "For I know the thoughts that I think toward you, saith the LORD, thoughts of peace, and not of evil, to give you an expected end" (Jeremiah 29:11). However, He does expect obedience. ". . . to obey is better than sacrifice . . ." (1 Samuel 15:22). In preparing our sons for the responsibility of providing for their families, may we teach them first and foremost to seek the Lord, following His direction.

## The Joy

There is joy in a parent's heart watching a son become the man God intended him to be. Part of that joy comes from knowing your son is prepared to support the family God gives him. This preparation should have involved leading him to salvation and spiritual maturity, instilling in him a hunger to serve others, and encouraging godly character growth—all necessary pieces of a man's ability to provide for a family. You have also been instrumental in developing good appetites in your son. The skills you have taught him and vocational training you have encouraged should stand him in good stead in the days to come.

May we be men and women of God, committed to investing our lives in the lives of our sons. May we be willing to make personal sacrifices in order to model the character and work ethic that will make our sons successful in their jobs. May we not introduce bad appetites in our sons, and may we starve our own bad appetites. May we truly, in every way, prepare our sons to provide for a single-income family!

# Additional Resources

---

**www.Titus2.com**—The official *Managers of Their Homes* website. You will find helpful samples of chore charts from many different families, information regarding all of our books, the most current Dad's and Mom's Corners, Steve and Teri's speaking schedule, and much more. To receive free monthly Dad's and Mom's Corners (written by Steve and Teri) via e-mail, just stop by the site and sign the guest book.

**www.PreparingSons.com**—The purpose of PreparingSons.com is to encourage fathers and sons in the Lord Jesus Christ. It is to be a clearinghouse for ideas, where fathers and sons can share with others who are like-hearted. A partial list of topics include:

- Building up sons to be men of God,
- School and Bible study project ideas,
- Developing vocational skills,
- Training and job opportunities,
- Testimonies.

# *Managers of Their Homes*
### A Practical Guide to Daily Scheduling for Christian Homeschool Families
### By Steven and Teri Maxwell

A homeschool mother's greatest challenge may be "getting it all done." *Managers of Their Homes* offers solutions! Responses by families who have read *Managers of Their Homes* and utilized the Scheduling Kit indicate the almost unbelievable improvements they have realized.

Step-by-step instructions and a unique scheduling kit make the setting up of a daily schedule easily achievable for any home-schooling family. *"People have told me for years that I need a schedule, but every time I tried I couldn't get one to work. I always had problems fitting everything that needed to be done into one day. With your system, I am actually accomplishing more, and I have more time left over! The key to it is the great worksheets. They are invaluable."* Who wouldn't like to accomplish more and have time left over?

*Managers of Their Homes, A Practical Guide to Daily Scheduling for Christian Homeschool Families* sets a firm biblical foundation for scheduling, in addition to discussing scheduling's numerous benefits. Chapter after chapter is filled with practical suggestions for efficient, workable ways to schedule a home-schooling family's days. Thirty real-life schedules in the Appendix give valuable insight into creating a personalized schedule.

*"My schedule has given me back my sanity!! I can't believe the way my life has changed since implementing a schedule."* Tracy L.

*"I had read almost every organizational book there was, and I still couldn't get to where I wanted to be until I applied this method!"* Corrie

*"In retrospect, having used the book, I would have paid $100 for it, if I could have know beforehand the tremendous benefits I would gain: peace in my busy home, and the ability my schedule gives me to accomplish the things I feel God wants me to do in my family."* Tracy

Perhaps *Managers of Their Homes* will provide solutions for your "getting it all done" challenges!

**For information visit: www.Titus2.com**

**Or call: (913) 772-0392**

# Just Around the Corner
### Encouragement and Challenge for
### Homeschooling Dads and Moms
## By Steven and Teri Maxwell

*Just Around the Corner* is a compilation of Steve and Teri Maxwell's monthly Dad's and Mom's Corners. These articles were originally written to encourage and support their local home-school group. However, they have been so well received that they are now requested via e-mail every month by thousands of home-school families.

The Maxwell's have also been asked to put the Corners together into this convenient-to-read book format. You will find the Mom's Corners grouped together in the front of the book and the Dad's Corners in the back. The Corners are all indexed so that you can read the ones relating to a specific topic you are interested in, if you so choose.

Because most of these articles deal with family life in general, many Christian non-homeschool families find them useful as well. Topics addressed in *Just Around the Corner* include: anger, depression, child training, husbands loving their wives, and wives submitting to their husbands.

Steve's writing will challenge dads in their role as the spiritual head of the family. Teri's writing addresses many aspects of daily life that often frustrate or discourage a mom.

With three of the Maxwell children now being adults, Steve and Teri write from the perspective of having seen the truth of God's Word put into practice. At the same time, they are still in the trenches homeschooling five children. You will have a candid vantage point as you see them fail, succeed, laugh, and cry while they endeavor to serve the Lord Jesus Christ.

Now you can enjoy the support and insights found in this unique, indexed collection containing six years' worth of Dad's and Mom's Corners.

**For information visit: www.Titus2.com**

**Or call: (913) 772-0392**

# Homeschooling with a Meek and Quiet Spirit

### By Teri Maxwell

Homeschooling moms are a wonderful group of women! There isn't a more determined, dedicated set of women in the entire world! These ladies have chosen an unpopular, difficult path that comes with little outside encouragement. Yet, they have set their faces on obedience to the Lord and what they know is best for their children—no matter what it costs them personally!

Even so, there are issues homeschooling brings up that are very common to most who homeschool. These common issues speak of what happens inside a heart when mom becomes responsible for her children's education, when they are home with her all day every day, and when she adds several hours' worth of homeschooling into a full schedule as a wife, mother, homemaker, and Christian.

A desire of a homeschooling mother's heart is to have a meek and quiet spirit instead of the discouragement, fear, and anger she often experiences. She can cope with the myriad of daily difficulties and decisions that a homeschooling lifestyle brings with it, as long as she is having the right responses to them. Let her be fearful, worried, anxious, frustrated, irritated, or angry, and this mom realizes she is undermining all she wants to accomplish by home-schooling.

Because Teri Maxwell has walked the homeschooling path for many years, she knows first-hand the struggle for a meek and quiet spirit. The memories from her early homeschooling years of often being worried and angry rather than having a meek and quiet spirit are unpleasant. Her prayer is that as she shares the work the Lord has done in her heart, through homeschooling, you would be encouraged that He can do the same for you. She also desires that you could learn from the lessons He has taught her so that you would begin to have a meek and quiet spirit long before she did.

Will your journey toward a meek and quiet spirit be completed upon finding the perfect spelling curriculum or deciding which chores your child should be doing? Or does the answer lie on a different path? In these pages, Teri offers practical insights into gaining a meek and quiet spirit that any mom can apply to her individual circumstances. She transparently shares the struggles God has brought her through and what He has shown her during these many homeschooling years.

In *Homeschooling with a Meek and Quiet Spirit*, you will discover the heart issues that will gently lead you to a meek and quiet spirit. Come along and join Teri as you seek the Lord to homeschool with a meek and quiet spirit!

**For information visit: www.Titus2.com**
**Or call: (913) 772-0392**

# *A Summer with the Moodys*
### By Sarah Maxwell

*A Summer with the Moodys* follows a family throughout the summer. You will see them help a widow and her dog, Honey. Max, Mitch, and Mollie start two little businesses. With those businesses come some excitement! Little Maddie adds her spark of joy, too. Woven throughout the book is the Moodys' love for the Lord and their fun time together. Commenting favorably on her children's enthusiastic response to the Moodys, one mom shared, "It's not very often that my kids come to me and ask things like, 'Mom, can we have Family Fun Night where we play games instead of movie night Friday?' or, after reading Scripture, 'Can we each pick out a way to apply that?'" This is not an adventure book, but rather a family-centered story with godly role models and Christian values.

**For information visit: www.Titus2.com**
**Or call: (913) 772-0392**

# Notes

————————————————

# Notes

# Notes

---

# Notes

_____